FURNITURE-MAKING

from the Inside Out

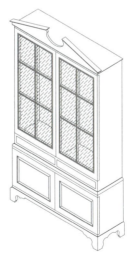

FURNITURE-MAKING
from the Inside Out

J.D. Lawrence

STERLING PUBLISHING CO., INC.

NEW YORK

Library of Congress Cataloging-in-Publication Data

Lawrence, J.D. (James D.)

Furniture-making from the inside out/J.D. Lawrence.
    p.   cm.
Includes index.
ISBN 0–8069–8566–6
1. Furniture making—Amateurs' manuals.
2. Cabinetwork—Amateurs' manuals. I. Title.
TT195.L38   1995
684.1'6—dc20   95–20391
                                            CIP

1   3   5   7   9   10   8   6   4   2

Published by Sterling Publishing Company, Inc.
387 Park Avenue South, New York, N.Y. 10016
© 1995 by James D. Lawrence
Distributed in Canada by Sterling Publishing
c/o Canadian Manda Group, One Atlantic Avenue, Suite 105
Toronto, Ontario, Canada M6K 3E7
Distributed in Great Britian and Europe by Cassell PLC
Wellington House, 125 Strand, London WC2R OBB, England
Distributed in Australia by Capricorn Link (Australia) Pty Ltd.
P.O. Box 6651, Baulkham Hills, Business Centre, NSW 2153, Australia
Manufactured in the United States of America

Sterling ISBN 0–8069–8566–6

This book is dedicated, with love, to those who's prodding and encouragement helped me to bring this work to fruition. They include my wife, Rebecca, son Joey, and daughter Leslie.

In addition, there was that very special kind of confidence that only a mother can convey. I shall forever regret her departure from this earth before I could complete the book she showed such enthusiasm for and present her with the copy she wanted.

Acknowledgments

The production of this book would not have been possible without the very gracious support of the following companies who provided material support and inspiration:

> Autodesk, which provided the AutoCad software used to generate all of the drawings in this project.

> The drawings were processed for publication using AutoSET Studio software.

> Bridge City Tool Works, 1104 N.E. 28th, Portland, Oregon 97232

> Delta Machinery International

> Garret Wade Company, Inc., 161 Avenue of the Americas, New York, New York 10013

> Woodcraft Supply Corp., 210 Wood Country Industrial Park, P.O. Box 1686, Parkersburg, West Virginia 26102

All of these companies are among the best in their field. Their willingness to support this project is especially meaningful to me.

Last, but not least, I would like to express appreciation to Sterling Publishing Company for their patience.

CONTENTS

FURNITURE-MAKING
MAKING
from the Inside Out

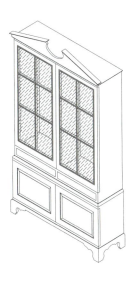

INTRODUCTION

Many people have told me that they'd like to build their own furniture, but were afraid they lacked the necessary skills. Skills are the fruit of seed sown of interest and nurtured with practice. They are only achieved by developing an understanding of the topics involved and practicing the techniques used.

How many times have you looked at a piece of furniture and thought "I surely would like to build one like that someday," only to put it off because you thought it would be too difficult? This happens a lot more often than most people want to admit, but this isn't necessary. Even the most complex furniture is little more than an assembly of component parts. Simply put, more complex furniture requires more parts that need to be built and assembled. When you think about it, the most complex furniture isn't any more difficult to build than the component parts that go into it.

To understand the construction of a piece of furniture, we first have to understand its component parts. This is the purpose of this book: to demonstrate how to break a piece of furniture into its component parts, build them from the inside out, and assemble them into a finished project. A common project might involve a carcass, face frame, doors, drawers, base frame, drawer support frame, and bracket feet. When these basic component parts are recognized and their construction understood, you can get started on a project with confidence. Of equal importance is to know how to join these component parts together to form the finished piece. You also could design your own projects by assembling the necessary component parts or building blocks to suit your needs.

As each of the component parts is discussed, I'll present several ways to build it. The idea is for you to study the various methods and decide which would work best for you. The selection of joinery is based on several factors. There is very seldom a "right" or "wrong" joint to use. The merits of each joint are discussed, so you can decide which ones you want to use. It's always a good idea to stop by the lumberyard and get some pine or other inexpensive material on which to practice. (Just make sure the pieces you work with are as free of knots as possible.)

Whenever possible, I'll cover both machine and hand-tool methods. I'd like to point out that the "traditional" joints become such because of a long, proven history. Traditions evolve as a successful method is handed down over several generations. There is value in the more traditional ways just as in the more modern methods, so don't discount them just for the sake of taking the modern approach.

The general category of furniture we'll cover is referred to as *casework*. The casework system of making furniture involves such projects as kitchen cabinets, bookcases, entertainment centers, wardrobe or gun cabinets, chests of drawers, etc.

In the following chapters I describe how to make the major components for a bookcase. A bookcase was selected because it contains the widest variety of component parts. You'll be able to see how each contributes to the finished piece of furniture. One very important point: *Although a bookcase is used as an example, the parts that it is made of are universal throughout the craft and can be used on any project. The bookcase is simply a study aid to show the relationships between the parts.* However, since no project is made of *all* possible components, we'll discuss these additional components and some applications where they can be used.

There are few activities as rewarding as applying your best efforts to quality material in its most basic form and ending up with a beautiful and useful piece of furniture that you and others can enjoy for years to come. Perhaps your children will pass that bookcase, and the story of how you built it, on to their grandchildren. It will also be the finest-quality furniture you'll possess. True solid hardwood furniture is rarely sold in furniture stores today. And when you do find it, you can bet it was not made with the same amount of loving care you would put into it.

J.D. Lawrence

FURNITURE-MAKING
from the Inside Out

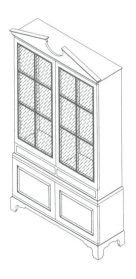

1 DISSECTING A PROJECT

Building a project such as the bookcase in Illus. 1-1 can be a real challenge. If you don't have a measured drawing or published plan, where do you start?

The job could be made a lot easier if the new cabinetmaker studied and understood the basic parts, or anatomy, of furniture. By studying furniture anatomy, you can start breaking the project into its component parts. Now isn't the time to be concerned with details of construction. That'll come later. For now, it's more important to get to know the major elements of construction. Then, study how to build each of them, one at a time.

When the bookcase is dissected according to its component parts, a drawing of the bookcase with its parts labelled can be developed, as shown in Illus. 1-2. The bookcase has two carcasses, a pediment, base, drawers, etc.; each of these major components can be broken down into individual parts. Only after all of the parts of the project have been defined, can construction begin. In the following sections, the major components of carcass furniture and their subcomponents are discussed.

Remember, as the complexity of the pro-

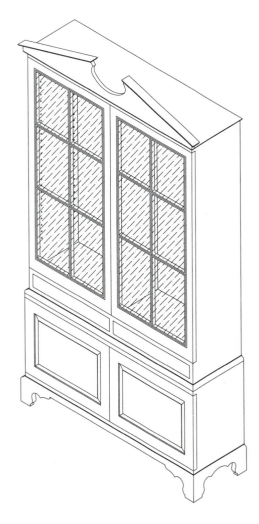

Illus. 1-1. The completed bookcase.

15

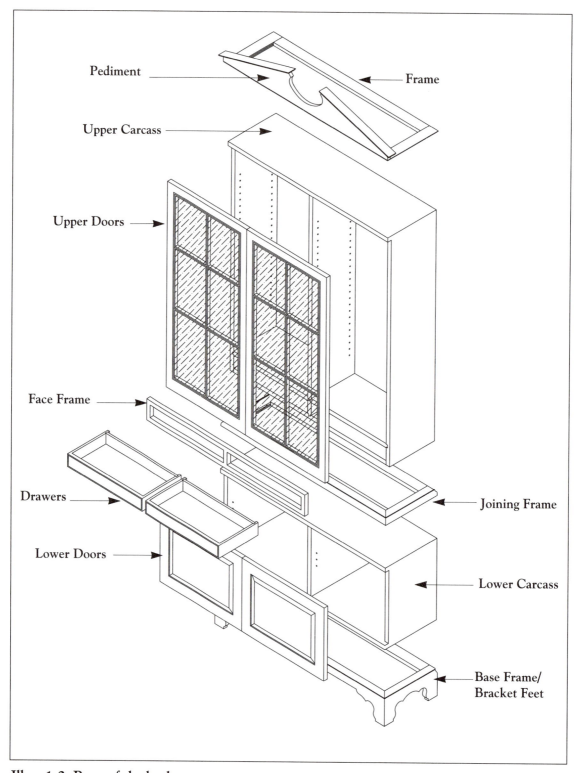

Illus. 1-2. Parts of the bookcase.

ject increases, more parts will need to be built. This is a very important point and is a key to building the confidence needed to venture into new, more complex projects. When looking at furniture, either in stores or catalogues, try to develop the exploded view drawing in your mind. As practice is gained "dissecting" furniture, you'll be more comfortable working with complex projects.

CASEWORK FURNITURE COMPONENTS

The carcass (Illus. 1-3) is the "shell" and forms the primary structure used in casework. It serves as a place to store things and provides support for all of the other components. The carcass has several components. *Shelves* can be either adjustable or fixed into place. *Partitions*

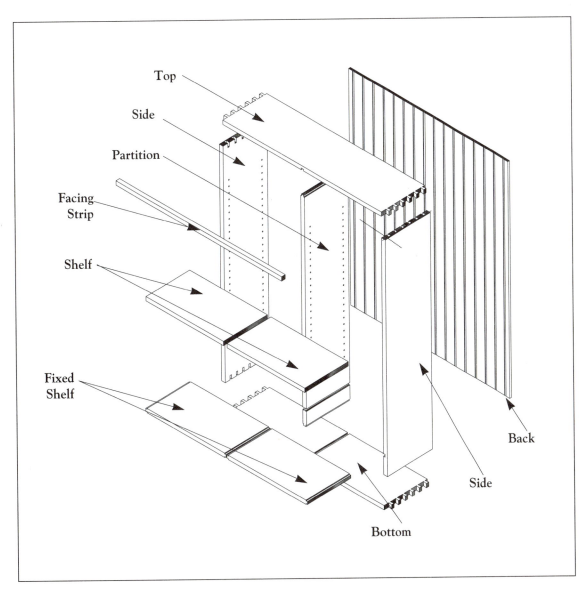

Illus. 1-3. Carcass.

are similar to fixed shelves except they are put in vertically. *Backs* can be either simple plywood panels or built up from boards. *Facing strips* are boards placed on the front of the carcass to provide separation between design elements or to step the front of the cabinet forward, as on the bookcase.

Sometimes the carcass opens from the top, such as a carcass on a blanket chest (Illus. 1-4). It's still basically a simple box.

A carcass may also be made of frame-and-panel construction. It's similar to a standard carcass except framed panels are substituted for the flat panels. These framed panels consist of vertical stiles, horizontal rails, and a panel let into a groove around the internal periphery. The panel can be raised or flat. Feet for a frame-and-panel carcass can be formed by extending the end stiles as shown in Illus. 1-4.

Internal frames (Illus. 1-5) are usually used to support drawers. Sometimes an internal frame is used at the top of the carcass and the top panel is attached to it. These frames are generally built of a front rail, two side rails, and a back rail. When drawers are to be supported, one or more intermediate rails may be added as drawer guides. Often, as with a chest of drawers, a dust panel is added by letting a ¼-inch sheet of plywood into the internal periphery.

Base frames (Illus. 1-6) are used on the bottom of the carcass and serve as a place to mount feet or attach a kicker board. A base frame is made of a front rail, side rails, and a back rail. For large spans, intermediate rails may be added.

Face frames (Illus. 1-7) are often added for style and additional structural strength. They also provide a convenient place to mount hinges when the doors don't extend to the carcass edge. Face frames are basic frames made up of vertical stiles and horizontal rails. Sometimes intermediate stiles and rails are also used. Face frames are commonly added to conceal the edges of plywood or veneered particleboard construction.

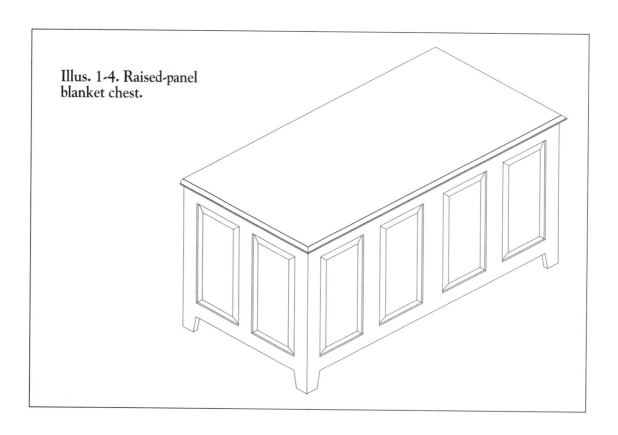

Illus. 1-4. Raised-panel blanket chest.

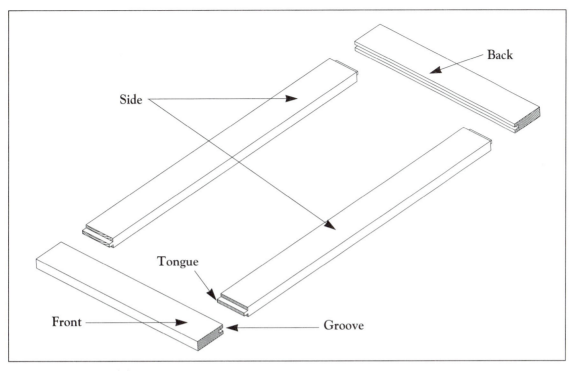

Illus. 1-5. Internal frame.

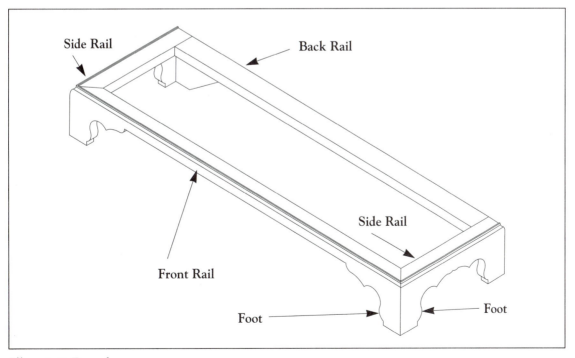

Illus. 1-6. Base frame.

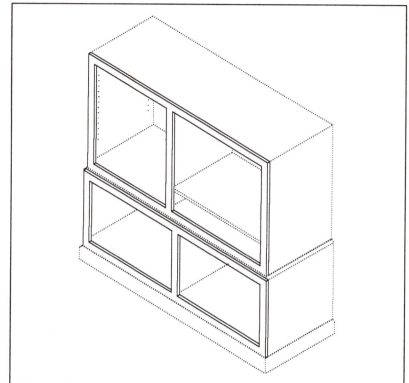

Illus. 1-7. Entertainment center with face frame.

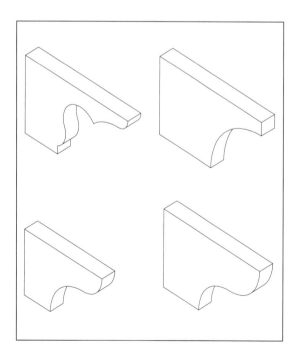

Illus. 1-8. Several bracket foot designs.

Bracket feet (Illus. 1-8) are often used on casework. They can be made in many shapes and are attached to the base frame.

Doors (Illus. 1-9) can take many forms. *Overlay doors* simply mount on the face frame and overlap the opening. An *inset door* is inset into the opening, but a lip still overlaps the edge. A *flush door* is completely set into the frame of the opening. It is usually flush with the frame or carcass. Flush doors require a stop to prevent them from going into the carcass. This is usually done by installing a fixed shelf at the top and bottom of the cupboard area, with the thickness of the shelf partially concealed by the facing boards. This arrangement ensures that the full cupboard will be open from top to bottom. *Fully inset doors* provide the greatest challenge because any fit error around the edge will be visible.

Doors can be either of simple panel construction or frame-and-panel. The frame-and-panel door (Illus. 1-10) is a door panel let into

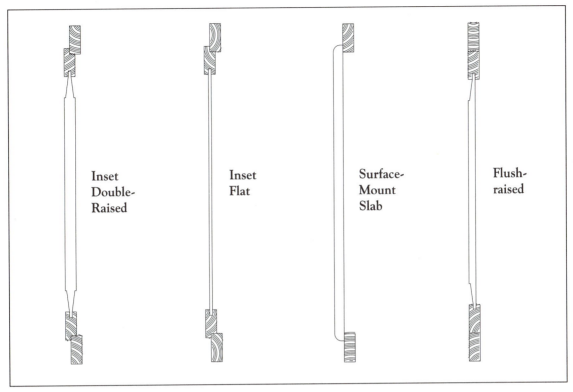

Inset
Double-
Raised

Inset
Flat

Surface-
Mount
Slab

Flush-
raised

Illus. 1-9. Cross-section views of several different types of door.

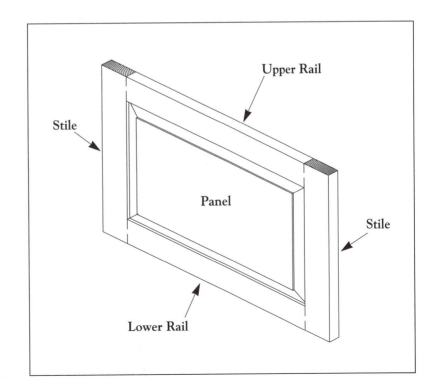

Illus. 1-10. Frame-and-panel door.

Upper Rail

Stile

Panel

Stile

Lower Rail

a frame constructed of vertical stiles and horizontal rails. Glass doors use a frame also. The panel is usually installed in a rabbet on the interior side. A *tambour door* is made from several slats and slides in a groove let into the side of the carcass. Tambour doors are most well known for use on rolltop desks.

Flip doors have been used for quite some time in the traditional "barrister's bookcase" (Illus. 1-11). They're becoming popular for use in entertainment centers and "video cabinets." Their ability to open and slide out of the way (Illus. 1-12) is favored by people (yours truly included) who think electronic equipment should only be visible when in use. (Face it, a lot of people would rather see a nice piece of mahogany or cherry furniture than a

television screen.) They can be used either vertically or horizontally.

Drawers (Illus. 1-13) can be mounted flush with their openings or they can overhang the openings. Sometimes the drawer will overhang on the top and sides, but not on the bottom. The front of the drawer is most often integral to the piece. Sometimes, a false front is applied to the drawer as either a board or frame and panel. When using flush drawers, remember to add a stop either on the drawer frame or carcass, to keep the drawer from sliding inside the cabinet.

The *entablature* is the decorative top put on the cabinet. It can take the form of a pediment, as on the bookcase as seen in Illus. 1-1, or it can be an applied cornice around the top of the case. (Illus. 1-14). The variety of shapes

Illus. 1-11. Barrister bookcase.

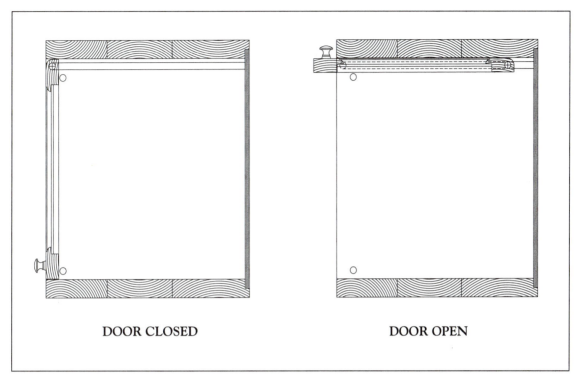

DOOR CLOSED   DOOR OPEN

Illus. 1-12. Flip door.

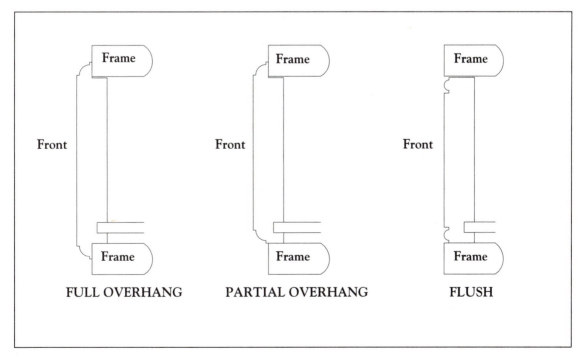

Frame   Frame   Frame

Front   Front   Front

Frame   Frame   Frame

FULL OVERHANG   PARTIAL OVERHANG   FLUSH

Illus. 1-13. Drawer types.

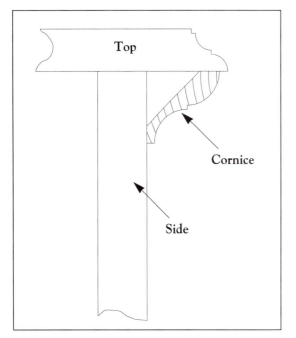

Illus. 1-14. Cross section of cornice.

Illus. 1-15. A finial.

is unlimited. Often, a cornice is used with a pediment to add flair. (Pediments are vertical boards set on top of a cabinet as design elements. They have no structural purpose.) Sometimes, finials are used with the pediment (Illus. 1-15). Finials are turned or carved features that are set into the pediment with a peg or dowel protruding from their base.

The basic components just described are found in all types of casework furniture, no matter what the design. Building a working knowledge of these parts will be a valuable investment as you develop furniture designs to suit your own needs. Once the general design is established, select the parts that'll be needed and arrange them in the fashion you select. It pays to study the various books and articles that discuss furniture design, especially if you want your project to fit into a particular, established style. ◘

2 WORKSHOP AND TOOLS

Before moving on to methods for building the individual parts of a furniture project, it would be a good idea to spend some time considering the workshop and tools needed. One of the first questions asked by the newcomer to the craft of woodworking is "What will I need in my shop?" Many have reached the conclusion that they'll have to put a third mortgage on the family home to buy the equipment. This really isn't the case. How much you spend on tools and equipment will be totally up to you. This chapter will provide some guidelines and help you get started.

We all adopt woodworking methods we're comfortable with, and too frequently find fault when others don't follow suit. In reality, there are very few absolute woodworking "rights" and "wrongs". Decisions regarding techniques involve cost, available shop space, personal skill level, and preferences, so don't be discouraged if someone criticizes your woodworking techniques. Remember, the important thing is results, not how you choose to get there. The methods discussed in the following chapters are presented in such a fashion that you can choose which one you prefer. Each method is equally effective, and has its own advantages and disadvantages.

The techniques involved in making furniture with the casework method range from working exclusively with just a few selected hand tools to operating a minifactory with tens of thousands of dollars worth of machinery. Working with hand tools does have its rewards. The sound of a plane slicing through seasoned lumber can be music to the ears. There's a level of control with hand tools that's absent with power tools. Power tools cannot make fine adjustments as reliably.

Some say it's inappropriate to use power tools when building furniture based on colonial American design. In fact, "power" tools date from the 18th century, when they were driven by large leather belts connected via shafts and gears to a water wheel.

Power tools do have their advantages. Possibly the most important is repeatability. Once a machine has been set up for a given task, you can repeat the operation any number of times confident that it will make uniform cuts. This is especially important when a project requires several similar parts. Power tools also allow a novice to do things that would take a great deal of practice to develop the skill required to do by hand.

In general, power tools are less time-consuming than their hand-powered counterparts. However, as experience is gained in the use of hand tools, many people find they get the job done by hand in the time it would take to set up many of the more complex power tools. Some people have physical limitations that would make working with some hand tools difficult, but are solved with a little help from a machine. I speak from personal experience in this area. Using a handsaw or sanding by hand can be very tiring for someone with limited endurance.

The most common problems with power tools involve cost and available shop space. Power tools are usually more expensive than hand tools. Often, there's a lot of time spent setting the machine up for even routine operations. Most machines require floor space that is at a premium in most home shops. The airborne dust that's generated often leads to the purchase of a dust collector to control it.

SAFETY FIRST!

Power tools and machines can be very dangerous if the safety rules aren't followed completely. Always read, understand, and follow the safety warnings included with the equipment. I know this is an often repeated warning, but too many people have been injured so seriously they're no longer able to or want to stay in the craft.

There are issues of safety that have to be addressed when using power tools. No matter how careful you are, a simple distraction or slip can result in losing a piece of anatomy nobody really wants to part with. Even though a dust collector is used, there will be a buildup of fine dust as it settles from the shop air. If not taken care of, this dust can significantly increase the fire hazard within the shop. The hazard with fine dust is much greater than with shavings generated by a plane. Flames spread much faster through particulate matter and are potentially explosive, depending on how the dust accumulates. Dust can also cause allergic responses, so be sure to use a dust mask if you're sensitive to it.

The potential for electrical fires is present anywhere machinery is used, so be sure to disconnect power at the end of the workday. Also, saws, routers, shapers, etc., throw a lot of debris. Be sure to wear safety glasses at all times. Another problem you can protect against is hearing damage caused by the noise coming from the machines (especially routers). Keep a good pair of hearing protectors handy and use them.

One final note on safety: Stay alert! Never operate machines when you have taken medications that may cause drowsiness or have drunk alcohol while working in the shop.

Don't be lulled into a false sense of safety when using hand tools, either. Although you might not be pulled into a spinning saw blade, cutting tools do just as their name implies. Chisels, carving tools, handsaws, and even plane irons can leave a cut serious enough to require emergency medical treatment.

Selecting Tools

Before you begin spending money on tools, read the following chapters and decide which ones you want to start with. When you're ready to buy your tools, be sure to invest in good-quality ones. Good tools, like the furniture they help you produce, will outlast their buyer and make a fine legacy to pass on to future generations. I like to subscribe to an old saying taught me by my father: "It's not how much you spend, it's how often you have to spend it." Buying a cheap tool and having to replace it quickly can be a very disheartening experience. We've all experienced this to some degree. This can be especially frustrating when talking about major machines such as table saws, etc.

As with anything else, we need to be smart consumers when buying tools. Always verify the reputation of the supplier/manufacturer. What's the policy for returns if you're not satisfied? This could be an important statement regarding a company's commitment to providing quality tools and customer satisfaction. Many woodworking and consumer magazines publish data comparing brand names of tools.

A word of warning when buying tools: Beware of unknown brands. Also, be aware that some mail-order sources and department stores put their own labels on inexpensive imports, and sometimes on high-quality tools to enhance their image in the marketplace. Copies are seldom of the same quality level as the original. This is what usually happens when someone sees a popular design and decides he could build and market it cheaper. If you don't recognize the manufacturer or if you think you see a bargain, make sure you'll be able to get spare or replacement parts. Also, make sure that there is a reliable service department in case you have a problem.

Be careful about buying tool sets. Although they may look like a good deal, they often have tools you may not need. For example, a set of four chisels is usually all the chisels you'll need. If you need additional sizes, you can order them individually. This will save a lot of money compared to initially buying a set of 12. I fell into this trap myself and have several tools I never use.

When ordering through the mail, you can't inspect the product personally. Always make sure you're dealing with a reputable source. Discuss the companies with friends who may have ordered from them. Find out how long they've been in business. The Better Business Bureau is also a good source of information.

BASIC WOODWORKING ACTIVITIES

Marking Out

Marking out is the process of measuring and marking the lumber for cutting. Tools involved are squares, marking gauges, and rules (Illus. 2-1). Squares are available as multi-purpose machinist's tools or specialized try, mitre, bevel, or dovetail squares. I haven't had much luck with the machinist's squares or cheap specialized models. They don't maintain the accuracy I demand. Some cheaper models aren't even square out of the package. Speaking of accuracy, tape measures generally have a built-in error that occurs when the hook on their ends move. A steel rule is best because it doesn't have the hook.

Preparing the Stock

Preparing the stock consists of flattening, cutting to thickness, or preparing one edge as

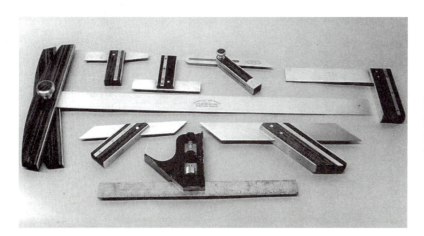

Illus. 2-1. Squares and marking gauges are used to measure and mark wood for cutting.

Illus. 2-2. Jack plane. *(Tool courtesy of Woodcraft Supply Corporation.)*

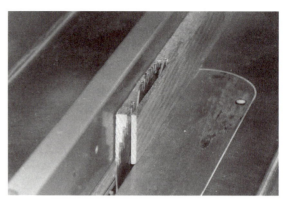

Illus. 2-4. Board being resawn on a table saw.

straight, square, and true as possible. You can usually order the wood at the thickness you need. The easiest way to flatten the stock is to buy good lumber to begin with that has been properly dried. If this isn't an option for you, you could use a hand plane (Illus. 2-2) or power planer (Illus. 2-3) to do the same job. You could also resaw the stock on a table saw (Illus. 2-4) or band saw. (Resawing is the process of cutting a thick piece of stock into two thinner pieces.) After resawing, you'll still

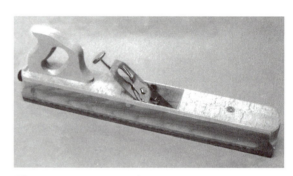

Illus. 2-5. Jointing plane. *(Tool courtesy of Woodcraft Supply Corporation.)*

Illus. 2-3. Power planer. *(Photo courtesy of Delta International, Inc.)*

Illus. 2-6. Jointer. *(Photo courtesy of Delta International, Inc.)*

need to dress up the surfaces with a plane to smooth and flatten it.

Straightening and squaring one edge is called "jointing." Jointing can be done with a jointing plane (Illus. 2-5) or a jointer (Illus. 2-6). It can also be done with a table saw, although not as well. Chapter 19 features a jig which can be used with a table saw. The jig acts as a carriage to move a piece of wood over the blade in a straight path without relying on the rip fence. It is also possible to order the stock "S1E" or "Straight One Edge," but this stock may not be absolutely square. S1E lumber usually requires dressing with either a jointer plane or a power jointer.

Dimensioning the Stock

The next operation would be to dimension the stock. It has to be crosscut to length and ripped to width. *Ripping,* or cutting along the length of the grain, can be accomplished with a handsaw (Illus. 2-7), table saw (Illus. 2-8), or band saw. The radial arm saw is *not* safe for ripping because the operator has to reach around the blade to push the stock through. Band saws may not give a straight cut because they were designed to cut curves.

Crosscutting, or cutting across the grain, can be done with a handsaw, table saw (Illus. 2-9), radial arm saw, or power mitre box

Illus. 2-8. Board being ripped on a table saw.

Illus. 2-9. Board being crosscut on a table saw.

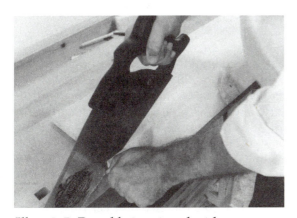

Illus. 2-7. Board being ripped with a handsaw.

Illus. 2-10. Power mitre box. (*Photo courtesy of Delta International, Inc.)*

Illus. 2-11. Router.

Illus. 2-13. Table-saw moulding head. (*Photo courtesy of Delta International, Inc.*)

Illus. 2-12. Shaper. (*Photo courtesy of Delta International, Inc.*)

(Illus. 2-10). The radial arm saw is usually limited to about a 16- to 20 -inch cut length and may not give a reliably square cut. Power mitre boxes have a very restricted cut capacity, although they were designed for accurate cuts.

Cutting Moulding

Moulding can be cut in several ways. Although routers (Illus. 2-11) and shapers (Illus. 2-12) are the power tools that are generally used, some moulding can be cut on the table saw (Illus. 2-13). The table saw has the disadvantage of being limited to straight edges. Moulding planes and scratch beaders (Illus. 2-14) are the hand tools for the task. These tools are not readily available on the market, except as antiques, and are expensive when found. There are very few moulding planes still manufactured. They are often more expensive than routers and router bits.

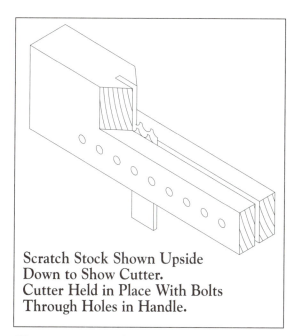

Scratch Stock Shown Upside
Down to Show Cutter.
Cutter Held in Place With Bolts
Through Holes in Handle.

Illus. 2-14. Scratch stock.

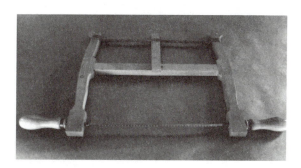

Illus. 2-15. Bow saw.

Both of the hand tools can be made in the home shop.

Cutting Curves

Curves can be cut by hand using a bow saw (Illus. 2-15) or coping saw. The coping saw is generally used for smaller parts. The sabre saw and band saw (Illus. 2-16) are the power tools used for the job. The band saw is the more expensive choice, and it requires shop floor space.

Illus. 2-16. Band saw. (*Photo courtesy of Delta International, Inc.*)

Finishing Preparation

There are a number of ways to prepare the project for finishing. The most common method is to sand the wood. Sanding can be done by hand or with a variety of power tools (Illus. 2-17). The belt sander isn't used very often for finish preparation, although the newer variable-speed belt sanders are more practical. You could also use cabinet scrapers or smoothing planes. Cabinet scrapers come in a variety of styles from a simple piece of metal (Illus. 2-18) to elaborate scraping planes (Illus. 2-19). Scrapers and planes leave the smoothest surface because they slice through the wood and remove the "fuzz."

Illus. 2-17. Palm and belt sanders.

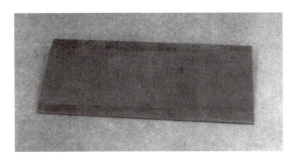

Illus. 2-18. A simple scraper.

Illus. 2-19. A cabinet scraper.

Carving Embellishment

Many furniture designs call for some carved embellishments. Carving can be an exciting hobby in itself. Carving tools often come in sets (Illus. 2-20). Remember the warning I gave you earlier. Start with a beginners set of six or so tools and buy special tools later as you need them. Most carvers do almost all of their work with fewer than 10 tools.

WORKBENCH

Whether you use power tools, hand tools, or a combination, a workbench is essential. It holds material securely as you work on it. There are a number of workbenches on the market if you want to buy one. They range from reasonably priced to very expensive.

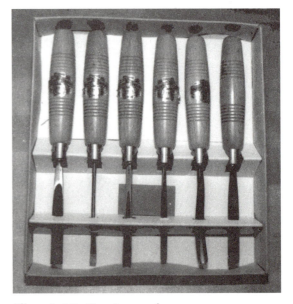

Illus. 2-20. Carving tools.

Illus. 2-21. Workbenches. (*Photo courtesy of Garret Wade Co., Inc.*)

Most people prefer to build their own to fit their particular needs. Illus. 2-21 shows a pair of workbenches; one also has a tool-storage cabinet. The workbench needs to be sized based on the work you are doing. Chapter 17 contains information on building a low-cost, functional workbench.

TOOL CHEST

You'll also need a place to store your tools. This can range from a simple crate to an elaborate furniture project. Either way, the tools should be easily accessible and secured when not in use. The tool chest is one of the most important projects made by many furniture craftsmen. Since no two people use the exact same complement of tools, it's nearly impossible to design a tool chest appropriate for every woodworker. I've designed a tool chest that is useful. It stores general-use tools. Chapter 16 contains information on building this tool chest. If you build it, you might consider adapting the design as necessary to accommodate your needs. The tool chest shown in Illus. 2-22 is a simple variation on the design. It, too, handles most small tools, but larger tools

Illus. 2-22. A completed tool chest.

such as saws will not fit. They could hang on a wall board.

ESSENTIAL WORKSHOP TOOLS AND AIDS

Whatever methods you plan to use to build your projects, there are tools and aids that are essential for any shop. Here's a list:

1. A good workbench to secure the wood as you work on it.
2. General-purpose chisels. (Start with a set of four.)
3. Marking squares.
4. Bevel square.
5. Marking gauge.
6. Dovetail saw.
7. Backsaw.
8. Rulers and or tape measures.
9. Straight edge for marking.
10. Mallet (wooden or rubber).
11. Block plane.
12. Smooth or jack plane.
13. Hammer.
14. Screwdrivers. (Make sure to use a screwdriver that fits the screw slot, to reduce risk of deforming the screw.)
15. Clamps.
16. A storage area for tools. Plans for a tool chest are in Chapter 16.

Power Tools

The common home shop is equipped with a *table saw* and *router*. These two machines are the busiest machines in most shops. The table saw is the most versatile workshop machine. It's crucial that you select a good one. Make sure the top is flat and cast iron, and that the motor or arbor carriage is strong and heavy. The heavier the better to reduce vibration that may make the cut rough. It's best to use a belt-driven machine because the motor will cause some vibration and the belt will reduce the vibration before it travels to the blade. The router should have at least 1½ horsepower and have the capacity for ½-inch shank bits. A dust collector (Illus. 2-23) is a good

Illus. 2-23. Dust collector.

investment because it controls dust buildup in the shop. Buy one that's rated at least 1 horsepower and 600 CFM (cubic feet [of air] per minute). A dust collector of this size is usually on casters and can be moved around the shop as needed. You can make a permanent dust collector installation by installing air flow ducts as required. Be sure to use metal duct material and ground it to eliminate static charge buildup caused by the airflow. A static spark could ignite the dust.

Even if you have decided to use power tools, consider trying a project with hand tools. It will prove to be an eye-opening experience. Most woodworkers end up using a combination of hand and power tools.

PERSONAL COMPUTER

A lot of woodworkers now use personal computers in their shop activities. The personal computer can be very useful in preparing drawings and construction plans for projects. Drafting and design software allow you to organize construction procedures and visualize how the project will look before you even begin to build it. Some packages, such as AutoCAD, although more expensive, are far better equipped to handle some drawing tasks involved in furniture design. Most of the less-expensive packages aren't capable of three-dimensional or isometric work.

Whether you use a personal computer or a pencil and paper, always prepare a complete set of drawings before making your first cut. This will give you a chance to ensure that all design factors are considered. ◙

3 THE CONVENTIONAL CARCASS

The *carcass* is the box or shell structure which forms the basis for casework furniture. A conventional carcass uses a single, wide, flat panel for the sides and top of the piece of furniture. It differs from the frame-and-panel carcass discussed in the next chapter in general construction technique.

Illus. 3-1 shows how our bookcase project is actually built up using two carcasses. Illus. 3-2 shows the parts of a basic carcass.

In it's most basic form, the carcass has a front, back, sides, top and bottom and is similar to a simple box. It can be transformed to accommodate specific needs simply by changing some of its parts, such as putting doors on the front (or top) and adding shelving and/or partitions inside. Drawers can also be added if needed. Study Illus. 3-1 to see how these parts might be assembled to form a more complex piece.

DETERMINING WHICH JOINTS TO USE

A wide selection of joints can be used in carcass construction. Historically, wood joints have been concealed from view. This was most common when working with dovetails and other intricate joints that might show some imperfection if done by hand. Today, however, many woodworkers like to display joints in their projects as design elements. The imperfections sometimes evident in hand-made joints usually don't show when the joints are made with power tools. But, to get the best decorative effect, it's best not to have the joints look like they were done by a machine. This is usually handled by avoiding repetitive, even spacing on dovetails and such.

As we discuss the use of joints in carcass construction, it's important to understand what makes some joints stronger than others. To understand where strength is needed most, it's a good idea to consider where the stresses are experienced by the structure. When these two things are considered, we can make better decisions when selecting which joints to use in a project.

The strongest joints are those that rely on a combination of glue bond and mechanical interlock between the pieces being joined. Therefore, the strongest joints in common use are the traditional dovetail and pinned mortise-and-tenon joints. Each of these joints has contemporary applications because of their

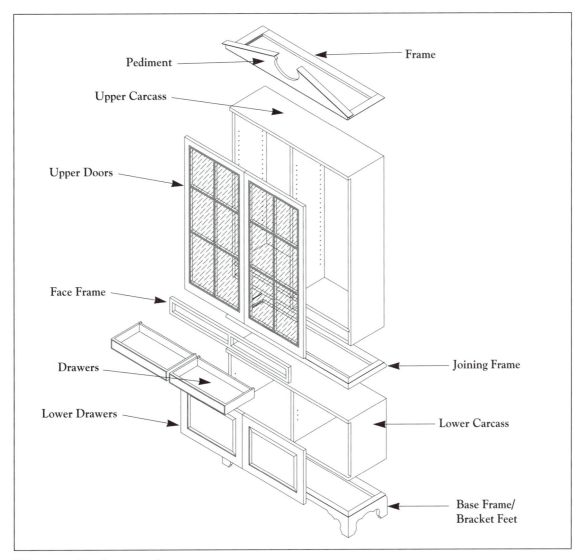

Pediment

Frame

Upper Carcass

Upper Doors

Face Frame

Joining Frame

Drawers

Lower Drawers

Lower Carcass

Base Frame/
Bracket Feet

Illus. 3-1. Bookcase with carcasses.

long-proven reliability.

For a strong glue bond, it's important to remember that end grain on wood does *not* take glue well. Modern glues work by forming a molecular bond with the wood. End grain has a very "open" texture that does not provide enough surface for an adequate bond. Edge or face grain provides the best surface for gluing. When the glue is "cured" (that is, has developed its strength and durability in the joint by undergoing a chemical reaction), the bond between mating parts is often stronger than the structural makeup of the wood itself. For the best glue joint, there should be a flush, tight fit between the two pieces. The glue bond will occur when the glue penetrates into the wood. This is why the joints on edge-glued panels with straightened and squared edges seldom require any additional treatment.

In understanding where carcasses need the most strength, we have to consider where and in what direction the joints will be stressed.

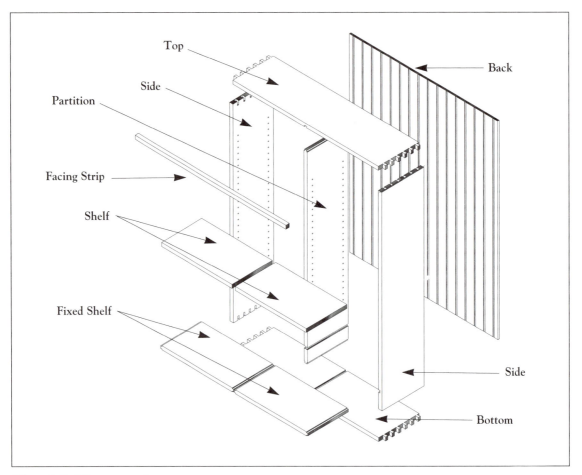

Illus. 3-2. The parts of a carcass.

For example, left alone, carcass sides would tend to fall out and away from the middle of the structure. Therefore, we would set dovetail joints so that the flared tails hold the sides to the top and bottom. On larger projects, the sides will tend to bow in the middle when the carcass is loaded down. For this reason, it would be best to use a sliding dovetail joint for fixed shelves or internal frames. A face frame would also provide added structure to the carcass to help prevent this bowing.

Edge-glued panels are used frequently in carcass construction. These panels are comprised of several narrow boards glued together. Even if we could find boards wide enough for our needs at the supplier, we're better off building them up. By building the panel of several narrow boards, we can minimize the cupping and warpage that occurs when the panels expand and shrink as the seasons change. Alternating the grain pattern of the pieces ensures that each piece will move independently (Illus. 3-3), offsetting adjoining pieces.

When starting to glue up a panel, take some time and study the boards you're going to use. Select your pieces for similar grain pattern and color. Ideally, the finished panel should look like one wide board. It should be flat and the joints unnoticeable. Remember that this is where the final appearance of the project can be made or ruined. A mismatched board will stand out (Illus. 3-4).

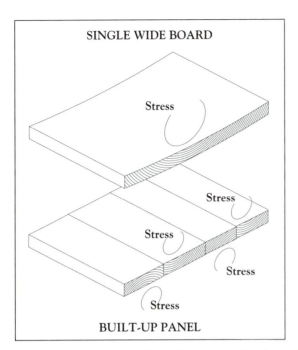

SINGLE WIDE BOARD

Stress

Stress

Stress

Stress

Stress

BUILT-UP PANEL

Illus. 3-3. The stress distribution in a built-up panel versus a single board.

Illus. 3-4. Badly matched boards.

As opposed to other joints used in furniture construction, the edge-glued joint relies entirely on the glue bond for strength. There isn't any interlock between the parts being fit together. This is satisfactory because edge grain is being glued to edge grain, and glue will form a very strong bond in this situation. The more area of edge grain covered with the glue, the stronger the joint will be. Some people would be tempted to use a tongue-and-groove joint or a spline (Illus. 3-5) to reinforce the joint. With the quality of modern glues, there is no need to use these joints, except in a couple of instances. First, they'll help to align the boards during the glue-up. This can be especially helpful when you are working with stock over 1½ inches thick. There are some species of wood, such as rosewood or lignum vitae, that have a high oil or resin content. These oils will prevent a really good bond. Although it helps to wipe the surfaces of these woods down with a solvent before gluing them, the spline will provide a larger surface area for the glue to bond to. Some thought needs to be

given to whether the end grain of panels employing splines or tongue-and-groove joints will be visible in the completed project. They can be obvious and harm the appearance of the project. They will also be visible when the panel is "raised" or moulding is made.

If you do not buy your wood S1E (Straight One Edge), you'll probably have to rip one edge of the boards straight. Chapter 19 contains information on making a jig that can be used with a table saw. This jig will help by acting as a carriage that holds the stock securely as it is guided over the saw blade.

JOINTING BOARDS

After the boards have been selected and arranged, it's time to *joint* them, that is, to straighten and square their edges. The goal is to have a joint with parts that are flush and in contact along the entire area of joint.

Jointing can be accomplished by several techniques. The most common one today is to use a motorized jointer. This is a machine with a long bed, rotating knives, and a fence to keep the board square with the cutters. Jointers range drastically in price and capabilities. All of them require floor space in the shop. When using a jointer, be careful to feed the wood with its grain (Illus. 3-6), and to do it slowly. The edge of the board needs to be smooth as well as straight. If the board is not fed correctly, the jointer cutters will "grab" the grain and tear it off. If fed too quickly, the board's edge will have a scalloped surface (Illus. 3-7).

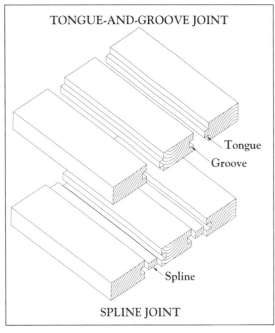

Illus. 3-5. Tongue-and-groove and spline joints.

The traditional method of jointing is to use a jointer (Illus. 3-8) or trying plane. These are hand planes with a long base, about 24 inches. (The longer the base, the straighter the cut.) Always set the plane iron to make a very fine cut, and make sure it is square with the bottom of the plane. Keep the iron *sharp* and work with the grain of the wood. This will ensure a smooth cut without tearing.

When jointing with a jointer or trying plane, you have to make a number of passes over the length of the board. At first, the cut will be "hit and miss." This is because the plane is removing wood at the high spots and missing the low spots. When you get one long curl of shaving, you'll know the edge is straight. Although the jointing plane will require some practice to master, it is less expensive than a jointer and doesn't require the floor space. The resulting edge is also smoother because the plane slices through the wood, instead of taking a series of cuts.

Another method of jointing the edge of a board is to use the table saw and a bench plane. Make sure the table saw's rip fence is parallel with the blade and that the blade is sharp. Set the fence to take a very fine cut

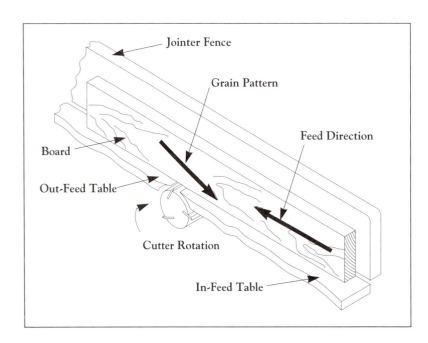

Illus. 3-6. Always feed the board with its grain into a jointer.

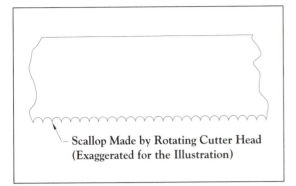

Illus. 3-7. If a board is fed too quickly into a jointer, its edges will have a scalloped surface.

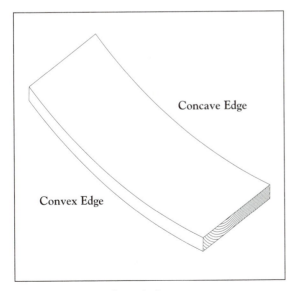

Illus. 3-8. A jointing plane.

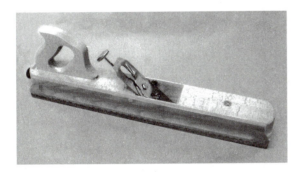

Illus. 3-9. Most boards have one concave and one convex edge.

(maybe ¼ of the width of the carbide tooth). Feed the stock slowly and carefully. Be careful not to feed so slowly as to cause the blade to burn the wood. Most boards have one concave and one convex edge (Illus. 3-9). You can see this better by sighting down the edge of the board. Run the concave edge of the board along the fence. This will ensure that the board will contact the fence in at least two areas. The convex edge won't follow the fence as well and the resultant cut could end up duplicating the curve you were trying to eliminate. For longer boards, you can extend your fence with some straight stock (Illus. 3-10). The result will be a fairly straight cut, but depending on the condition of the blade, it'll probably need to be dressed up with a smoothing or jack plane. Make sure the plane iron is square to the body, and take very fine shavings.

GLUING UP THE PANEL

Now that the parts are ready, it's time to glue up the panel. Start by arranging the pieces as described earlier. Spread a thin layer of glue along the edges of both boards. Make sure the glue covers the entire surface. Use pipe or bar clamps on alternating sides of the panel. Use

Illus. 3-10. A fence extension.

Illus. 3-11. A clamped panel.

just enough clamp pressure to squeeze out a line of glue from the joint. Alternating the clamps ensures a better distribution of the clamping pressure and a flatter panel (Illus. 3-11). Start at one end and tighten the clamps as you work to make sure the boards are as level as possible.

After the glue has cured, remove the clamps in reverse order from how you applied them. Use a scraper to remove the glue squeezed out. Don't try to sand it off. The glue will only gum up the sandpaper. It isn't very often that the panel will come out of clamps perfectly level (Illus. 3-12).

When the glue has been removed, use either a plane or sander to level the surface. A lot of people will use a belt sander for this job. Be careful! Belt sanders can remove a lot of wood in a hurry and gouge the panels beyond repair. Work slowly and deliberately with a belt sander. Always keep the sander moving, to avoid "dishing" the surface. Practice on some scrap before using it on your good stock. Start the tool before you put it down on the work, and be sure to always keep the sander flat on the work and to not put it down or lift it up by an edge or at the roller.

Don't try to force the sander by applying weight; let the weight of the tool do the work. Always work a belt sander with the grain of the

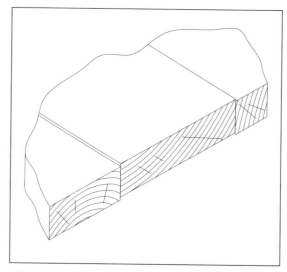

Illus. 3-12. An elevated board.

wood, or move the sander first diagonally and then sand with the wood's grain. Use the finest grit you can, to avoid taking off too much. If you use a belt sander, bear in mind that you'll probably have to sand again with a finer grit to remove the marks it leaves behind.

The hand-tool method is to remove the high spots with a jack plane and finish levelling

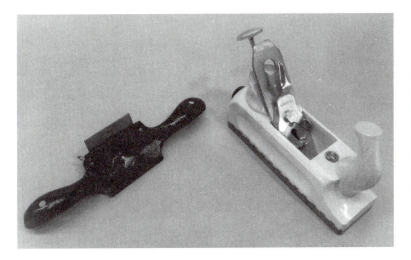

Illus. 3-13. To level the surface of the wood by hand, first remove the high spots with a jack plane, shown at right, and finish levelling the surface with a smoothing plane or cabinet scraper, shown at left.

the surface with a smoothing plane or cabinet scraper (Illus. 3-13). It might take a little longer to level the surface, but you'll have better control over what you're doing. When removing high spots, such as where a pair of boards don't match, make a skew cut at a diagonal to the grain and dress up the area with some light cuts with the grain. A "skew" cut is one where the plane is held on a slight diagonal to the direction it is moving. Keep your plane irons sharp and take thin cuts for the best results.

Some people will use both power- and hand-tool techniques to level the surface of wood. They start by levelling misaligned joints with a hand plane and finish up with a fine-grit belt on a belt sander.

There are wide-belt or drum-sanding machines that will level and smooth a panel up to 36 inches in one pass. These machines cost several thousands of dollars and use quite a bit of shop space. They really aren't for the home shop but, some cabinet shops or hardwood suppliers will put your panels through their machines for a fee.

ASSEMBLING THE PANELS

After the panels are prepared, it's time to start considering which joints to use to assemble them. The first group of joints will form the corners of the carcass.

Dovetail Joint

The most traditional joint used is the dovetail joint. It's a very old joint and is often considered a hallmark of quality craftsmanship. Dovetail joints are so named because they resemble the tail of a dove. A dovetail joint is strong because there is a mechanical lock between the two pieces of wood. A lot of area is also created for long-grain-to-long-grain gluing. The two most common dovetail joints are the through and the half-blind or lapped joints (Illus. 3-14). (Later, we will cover the sliding dovetail for installing fixed shelves, drawer frames, or partitions.)

Dovetail joints can be made in three ways: by hand, with a router, or on a table saw. It takes a bit of practice to be successful at making the joint by hand, but that is the traditional method. Before making them, however, you should understand some terminology and how to lay them out. There are two parts that form a dovetail joint: the tail and the pin.

There are two popular angles to use when designing the dovetail joint. They are 6:1 (for softwood) and 8:1 (for hardwood), or roughly 10 degrees and 8 degrees, respectively, as shown in Illus. 3-15. These angles were established well before America was even a group of colonies. They establish a good interlock between the parts, and prevent the parts from splintering off while being assembled. The 6:1

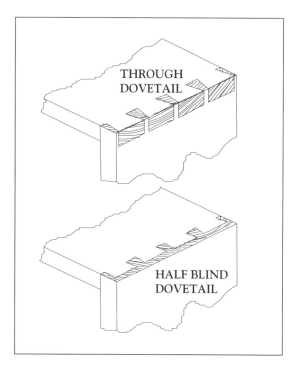

Illus. 3-14. Through and half-blind dovetail joints.

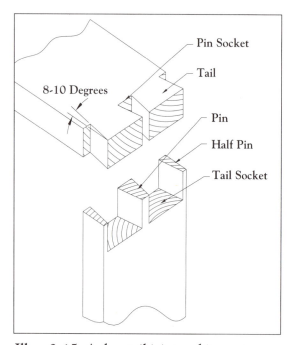

Illus. 3-15. A dovetail joint and its parts.

Illus. 3-16. A bevel guage being set for a dovetail joint.

and 8:1 references refer to how the bevel gauge is set to the angle (Illus. 3-16). Draw a line 8 inches long that is square with the edge of a board. Make a mark one inch offset from that line along the edge of the board. Now, place the handle of the bevel square against the board and set the blade to line up with the end of the 8 -inch line and the mark. The bevel gauge is now set up to lay out 8:1 dove-tail joints. You could buy special dovetail squares to do the job.

The next step in laying out the joint is to position the tails along the edge of the tail board. Start by marking the length of the tails across the end of the tailboard with a marking gauge. This length should be the same as the thickness of the pin board plus about $1/64$ inch (Illus. 3-17). The easiest layout would be to start with a half pin on the ends, divide the center portion into equal parts, and lay out dovetails of uniform width. (Remember that the more pins we use, the more important the spacing of the pins is to achieve a good fit.) Mark the pin locations with an X, to avoid cut-ting out the wrong part later. Be sure to contin-ue the lines over the end of the board (Illus. 3-18). As practice is gained, the width and positioning of the tails/pins can be varied, for aesthetic reasons. Use the tail layout to mark the positions of the pins after the tails are cut.

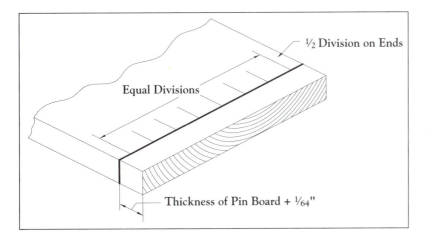

Illus. 3-17. Start of lay-out for a dovetail joint.

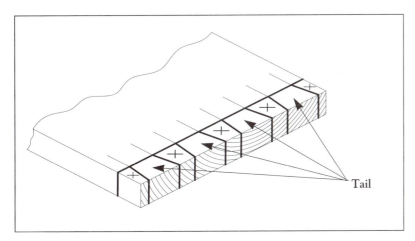

Illus. 3-18. Pin and tail layout. The pins are des-ignated by the letter X.

Illus. 3-19. The tail being cut.

Illus. 3-20. Use a chisel to clean up the cuts after you have removed the waste.

Cutting Dovetails By Hand

To cut the dovetail joint by hand, a dovetail saw, coping saw, and chisel are needed. Start by securing the tail board in a vise. Saw down the lines that separate the tails from the waste (Illus. 3-19). Be sure to saw on the waste side of the line. If necessary, the line can be smoothed up with a chisel later. Cut all of the tails. You might find it easier to set the board in the vise with the lines for one side of the tail vertical, cut them, reset the board, and cut the other side.

After these cuts have been made, the waste has to be removed. You could either do this with a chisel or a coping saw. If you use a coping saw, the waste piece won't break off and jam itself into the wood. After you saw the waste pieces free, use a *sharp* chisel to clean up the cuts with very light paring cuts (Illus. 3-20).

Now, use the tail board to mark the pin board. Cut the pins the same way you cut the tails, but don't rush it. Remember, it's easier to trim a little later than to have to start over because the pins aren't wide enough.

Try to fit the parts together. Mark where you need to trim the tails or the pins and make very fine cuts with a sharp chisel. Continue this until the parts fit together.

Cutting Dovetails With a Table Saw

Cutting the dovetails with a table saw will help the beginner get straighter, smoother, and more accurate cuts. The only drawback to using a table saw is that it is limited to cutting through dovetails. You'll have to mark the cut lines on both sides of the board and make a couple of jigs to attach to the mitre gauge of the saw (Illus. 3-21). Make sure that the vertical member is high enough to support your stock. Except for marking both sides of the board, the layout is the same as for cutting by hand. Since you'll be handling the boards vertically, you'll have to limit their length to something you can handle.

To cut the dovetails, set the blade to the angle of your choice and raise it to the layout line. Be sure to allow for the thickness of the jig (Illus. 3-22). Set the table saw's mitre gauge square with the blade. Now, attach the jig to the mitre gauge and pass it over the blade. Use the cut in the jig to position your stock. Again, be sure to cut on the waste side of the layout lines. When you have cut all of the marks on one side, rotate the board to cut the other side. Remove the waste stock with a coping saw and trim the pockets with a chisel.

To cut the pins, remove the jig from the

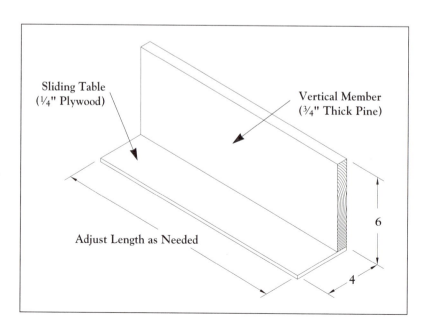

Illus. 3-21. Jigs used to make dovetail joints on a table saw.

Sliding Table (¼" Plywood)

Vertical Member (¾" Thick Pine)

Adjust Length as Needed

6

4

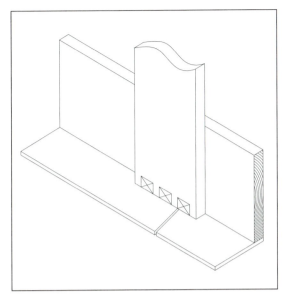

Illus. 3-22. The board in the jig is ready to cut the tails of a dovetail joint.

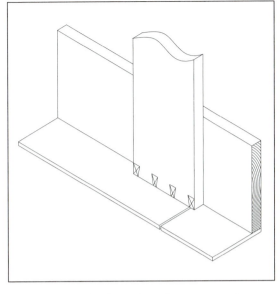

Illus. 3-23. The board in the jig is ready to make the pin cuts.

mitre gauge and attach a fresh one. Set your bevel square to the same angle as the blade relative to the table. Now, set the blade square to the table and use the bevel square to reset your mitre gauge. You'll need to reset the height of the blade after squaring it. Pass the jig over the blade as before and make your pin cuts (Illus. 3-23). Remove the waste stock and trim the pockets. Now, check the fit of the joint and do any necessary trimming with light cuts using a sharp chisel.

Another popular dovetail joint is the *half-blind* joint. It is called half blind because only one side of the joint can be seen. Its most common application is in building drawers. The tails are cut just as in through dovetails, except that they are shorter and cut first. The difference lies in the pin cuts.

Start by laying out the joints and cutting the tails. The tails should be about three-fourths the thickness of the pin board (Illus. 3-24). Obviously, this may change as other situations demand. Mark a line to match the thickness of the tail board.

Use the tails to mark out for the pins. This can be awkward if you don't have a bench

with a front vise. You would be better off placing the pin board in a vise.

The pins are usually shaped completely by a chisel. Be sure to use a *sharp* tool. Start by outlining the cut. Leave a little wood between the chisel and the layout line. You'll go back later

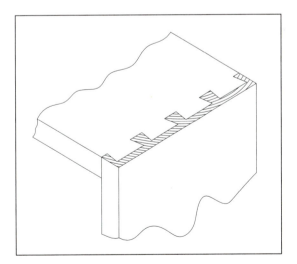

Illus. 3-24. The tail length for a half-blind dovetail joint.

and do final trimming. Now, go around and start removing the material. Work slowly and don't try to take out the entire depth of the cut in one pass, because the wood may split. After you've gotten to the bottom of the cuts, remove the rest of the stock just as before.

Cutting the Dovetail Joint With a Router and Dovetail Jig

The most popular method for cutting dovetails by machine is to use a router and dovetail jig. There are several dovetail jigs on the market. They cover a wide range of prices and capabilities. Most of the less-expensive jigs have the same shortcomings: they can only cut half-blind dovetails at a set pattern. Jigs that will cut through dovetails are more expensive. I only know of one manufacturer that builds a jig system that will cut both through and half-blind dovetail joints and allow you to adjust pin size and spacing.

This is where you have to decide whether to use hand tools or machines to make dovetail joints. If you're just starting out and don't have the time to develop the skills to cut dovetails by hand, or if you don't plan to do it often enough to maintain the skills, you would probably be better off doing it by machine. If you'll only be working with through dovetails and your projects will be of a size you can han-

dle, the table-saw method will do. The less-expensive dovetail jigs used with a router will be adequate for drawers and other small projects that have half-blind dovetails. If you're planning to use through and/or half-blind dovetails to join large carcasses as well as drawers, I suggest you consider spending the extra money for a more versatile jig system.

The router/jig dovetail systems come with their own instruction manuals. Read the manual! If a video is available from the manufacturer, I suggest you get one. They're great at covering some details overlooked in the text.

Box Joint

Another joint that resembles the dovetail is known as a *box joint* (Illus. 3-25). This joint was developed for factory production. It was used for small wooden boxes that were used to contain products coming out of factories, or for storage boxes (Illus. 3-26). A box joint has a lot of edge-grain glue surface, which adds to its strength. Some people call it a *finger joint* because when completed, it looks like interlaced fingers.

One disadvantage of this joint is because all of the fingers and their spacings must be uniform it looks like it was made in a factory. That's not necessarily bad unless you want the finished product to look handcrafted. It is most often used for utilitarian applications

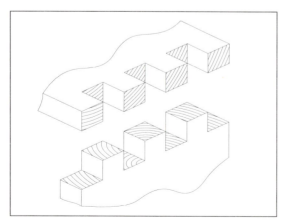

Illus. 3-25. A box joint.

Illus. 3-26. A box built with box joints.

rather than for decorative reasons. The fingers can only be cut as a through joint. There is no efficient way to make a half-blind finger joint.

After a couple of years of natural wood movement due to changes of seasons, the surfaces of the joints, along the edge, may not be perfectly level. This is perfectly natural because wood swells more in thickness and width than in length. The effect will be barely perceptible. The same could occur in similar joints such as through dovetails.

There are a couple of methods for making the box joint. One involves using a router. You'll need a router table with a slot to guide a jig (Illus. 3-27). A plan to build your own router table can be found in Chapter 18.

The jig is little more than a mitre gauge similar to that found on a table saw. Use a C-clamp to hold a facing board in place while you pass it over the router bit. (Be sure to use a pin spacing large enough to let you work inside it to apply glue.)

After the jig has been passed over the router bit, turn the router off and *very carefully* move the facing board over the exact distance as the width of the router cut. Take your time at this, to get the spacing accurate; if you don't, the joints won't fit properly.

Cut a block of hardwood to fit the original cut in the facing board. It should be long enough to extend slightly beyond the thickness of the stock you'll be jointing. Glue that block in place to act as a guide pin for positioning the stock in the jig.

Start the process of cutting the joints by setting the board in the jig as shown in Illus. 3-28. Make your first pass.

Now, set the stock over the guide pin and make your second pass. Continue until all cuts have been made.

When using the box joint, you'll note the joining boards need to have their fingers offset for a proper match. This is accomplished by making a little spacer block as shown in Illus. 3-29.

Take a scrap piece of stock and place it in the jig with one edge against the guide pin. This will give you a slot to place over the guide pin that is properly spaced from the edge of the stock. When making the first pass on the stock, use the spacer as shown in Illus. 3-30. Now, put the spacer away and complete routing the stock as before. Store that spacer in the tool chest and mark it as a *tool*.

The second method for preparing the box joint is to use a table saw with a dado blade.

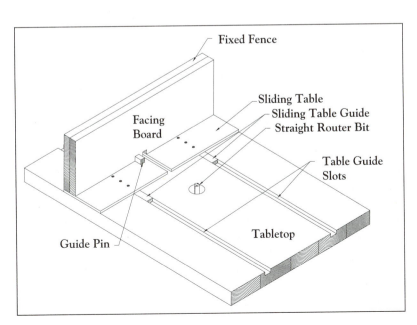

Illus. 3-27. Router-table-and-jig setup for cutting box joints.

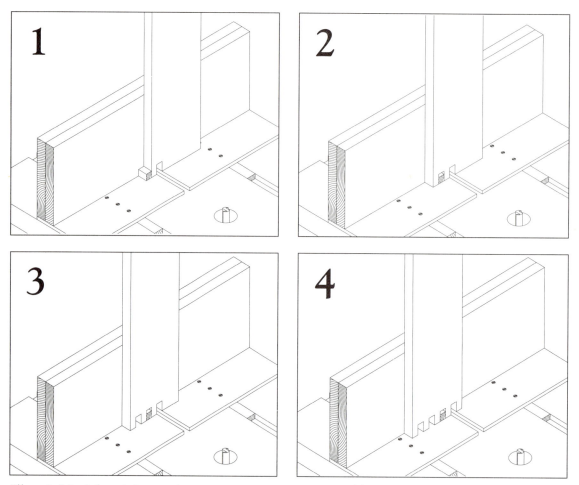

Illus. 3-28. A box-joint cutting sequence using a router table and jig.

The techniques are the same as with a router table. The only difference is the use of a different machine. The slots are cut on the table saw with a dado blade.

There are essentially three different variations of dado cutters. The first is the older *stacked dado set*. These are sets of blades, and the width of the dado is controlled by how the blades are "stacked up." They are usually limited to $\frac{1}{16}$-inch increments, ranging from $\frac{1}{4}$ to $\frac{13}{16}$ inch. The other two types of dado cutter are infinitely variable. They are generally referred to as wobble or Vee dado cutters.

Wobble dado cutters are adjusted by setting the blade to an angle relative to the arbor of the saw. The greater the angle, the wider the cut.

This adjustment is made possible by various methods, depending on the manufacturer, but, basically an adjustable hub that fits over the saw's arbor shaft is used to make the adjustment.

V-type cutters are comprised of two blades that are set at an angle to each other, forming a V shape. Their adjustment is similar to that of the wobble cutter. The angle of the V cutter sets the width of the cut.

There is a distinct difference between the stacked dado set and the adjustable or infinitely variable dado cutters. Because of the way the adjustable cutters operate, the bottom of their cuts is not flat. It's radiused from the middle of the blade. The result is that the box joints will not fit together completely snug.

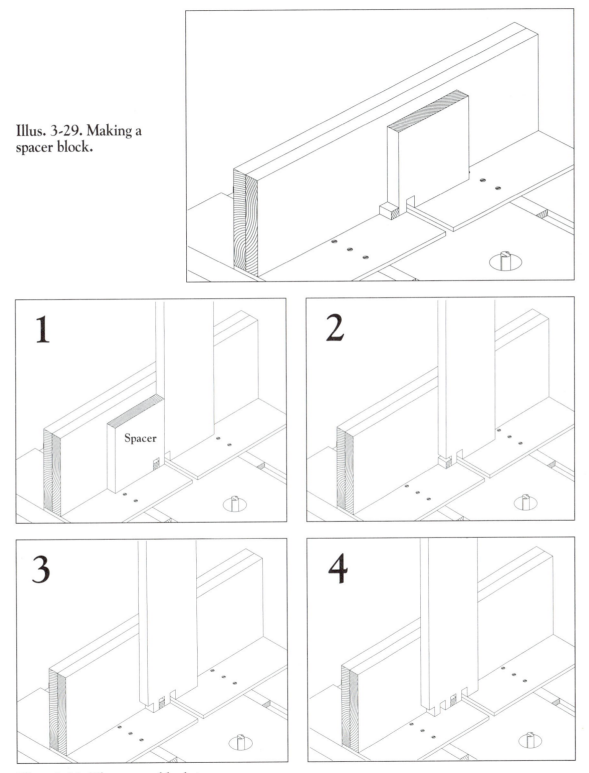

Illus. 3-29. Making a spacer block.

Illus. 3-30. The spacer block in use.

Sometimes, there will be a very visible gap. The severity of the gap will depend on the diameter of the blade and the width of the cut. A V-type dado cutter will provide a flatter bottom cut than the wobble dado cutter, but the cut will still be somewhat curved.

The stacked dado set is usually made up of two outer blades that are similar to ordinary carbide-tipped saw blades. A number of "chipper" blades are sandwiched between them to set the width of cut. These chipper blades usually have far fewer teeth than the outside blades and make a much coarser cut. To compensate, the outer blades are generally ever-so-slightly larger in diameter than the chipper blades. Although the stacked dado set does not yield a curved bottom, this difference in blade size could form an elevated section. More often than not, this effect is not visible after the joint is drawn tight with clamps for gluing.

The flattest bottom is obtained with the router table method.

Half-Blind Tongue-and-Rabbet Joint

The next joint we'll look at is the half-blind tongue-and-rabbet joint, as shown in Illus. 3-31. Although it provides some mechanical interlock, it isn't as strong as a dovetail joint.

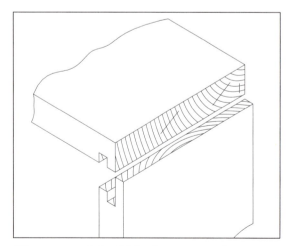

Illus. 3-31. A half-blind tongue-and-groove joint.

In this joint, long grain is glued to end grain, and, as mentioned earlier, end grain will not take glue very well.

Although the half-blind tongue-and-rabbet joint could be made by hand, it pretty much requires the use of a table saw. To keep the operation safe, you should use a tenoning jig as shown in Chapter 19. A stacked dado set will also help speed the cuts when you are working on thick stock.

Start your layout on the piece with the groove or rabbet. Mark dimension A as shown in Illus. 3-32 to two-thirds the thickness of the mating stock. Dimension B should be about one-third the thickness of the mating stock. Dimension C should be about one-third the thickness of the grooved part.

To cut the groove, set your stock on the table saw and raise the blade to the height of the C dimension. Use the marked-out stock to gauge the blade height. This will eliminate any error that can be introduced by a misread ruler. Using a small "sliding table" as done for box joints and table-sawn dovetails will give more accurate positioning of the groove. Simply attach the jig to your mitre gauge or make your own metal or hardwood piece to fit your mitre gauge slot. Pass the jig over the blade and you have an accurate reference with which to align your layout lines. There is a plan for such a jig in Chapter 19. You'll find it useful for just about all square cutoffs.

Use a tenoning jig to cut the part with the tongue. You can buy a tenoning jig or make one with plans provided in Chapter 19. To lay the tongue out, hold the stock against the grooved part as shown in Illus. 3-33. Mark the thickness of the tongue and the end of the grooved piece. Dimension A in Illus. 3-34 should equal the thickness of the grooved board, although it would be a good idea to make this dimension about 1/64 inch longer than the thickness of the grooved stock. When the joint is assembled, the tongue part will be slightly longer than the mating part and can be trimmed flush with a plane, scraper, or sander. It's a lot eas-

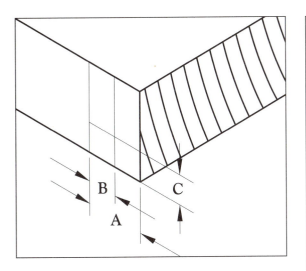

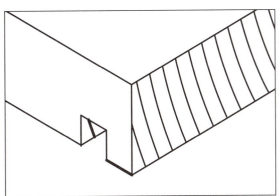

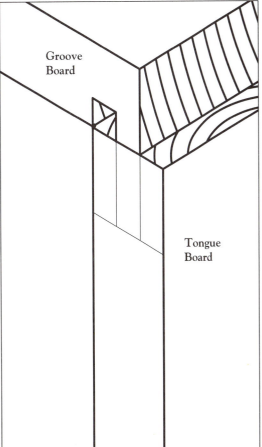

Illus. 3-32. The layout for a tongue-and-groove joint.

Illus. 3-33. When cutting the tongue, lay out the parts as shown here.

ier to trim that part than plane the grooved board to get a flush fit.

Use the grooved board to mark the line, to eliminate measurement error. Dimension C in Illus. 3-34 will establish the tongue. Measure the groove depth on the mating part carefully when laying it out. If it is cut too short, you will have a gap in the joint. If it is too long, the joint will not seat completely.

Use the old rule of measuring twice before cutting once. Use a tenoning jig to cut the groove, as shown in drawing 3 of Illus. 3-34. This is really the only safe way to cut the groove on a table saw. The cut can be made with either a standard saw blade or a stacked dado blade. If you use a single blade, you will

probably need to make more than one pass to get the thickness of the cut right. Again, raise the blade to the layout line on the stock rather than measuring with a rule, to ensure the best fit.

After the groove is cut, you can trim the tongue. You may want to make the first pass a little long, and then make additional fine trimming passes until you achieve a nice, tight fit.

Mitred Tongue-and-Rabbet Joint

Sometimes, in a smaller carcass, it would be nice to have corners with no end grain visible. A bevel mitre cut can be made in an offset tongue-and-rabbet joint to achieve this

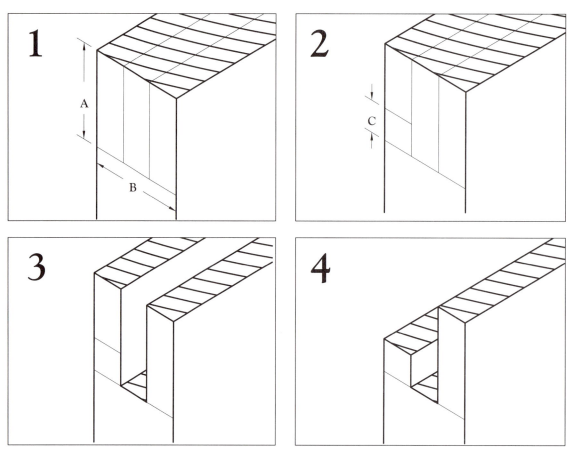

Illus. 3-34. The layout for a tongue-and-groove joint.

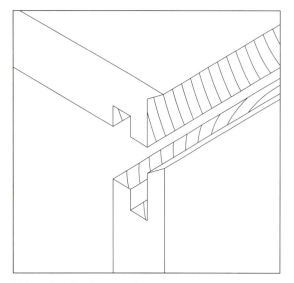

Illus. 3-35. A mitred joint.

(Illus. 3-35). The layout and cutting sequence is similar to that for the tongue-and-rabbet joint we just covered, with a couple of additional cuts.

Illus. 3-36 shows the process for making the groove board. You'll note the added mitre bevel on the end. Start laying out by dividing dimension A, the thickness of the mating piece, in three. Just as in the previous joint, dimension B is about one-third the thickness of this piece.

Illus. 3-37 shows that the tongue board is identical to that of the offset tongue-and-rabbet joint, with the added bevel mitre cut on the part that would otherwise extend over the end of the grooved or rabbeted board. ◙

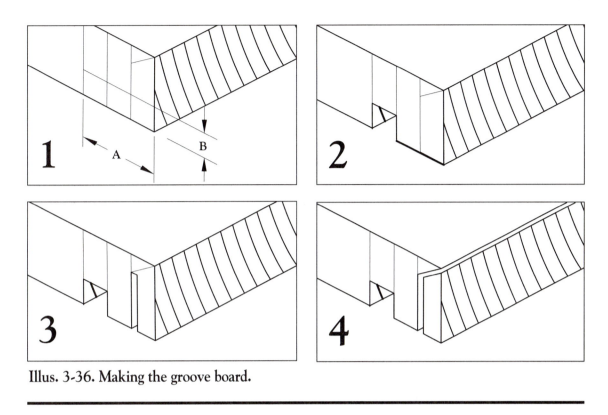

Illus. 3-36. Making the groove board.

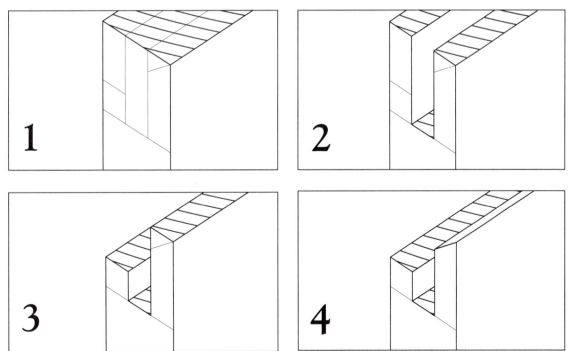

Illus. 3-37. Making the tongue board.

4 THE FRAME-AND-PANEL CARCASS

Not all carcasses are built using flat panel construction. There are times when frame-and-panel construction is chosen. Some people prefer frame-and-panel construction as a way to avoid cross-grain joinery. Illus. 4-1 shows a blanket chest made of frame-and-panel construction. Frame-and-panel construction allows for a very flexible design. This type of construction isn't any more difficult than conventional construction.

Illus. 4-2 shows the parts of a frame-and-panel carcass. The panels, which can be either flat or raised, are let into grooves in the frame members. They are usually oriented with their grain running along their long axis. The frames are built up with horizontal rails and vertical stiles. Depending on the size of the carcass, additional stiles and rails may be added. Appropriately enough, they are called intermediate stiles and intermediate rails. The blanket chest shown in Illus. 4-1 has several intermediate stiles that support the vertically oriented panels. It could be built with one large panel installed horizontally if you wish. Just remember that the structural support for the frame-and-panel construction is in the frame. The panels provide no structural support.

THE FRAME

Building the frame-and-panel carcass involves many of the same techniques as building frame-and-panel doors. Following is information on how to build the frame.

Mortise-and-Tenon Joint

The traditional joint for frame construction is the mortise-and-tenon joint. It's very strong and is easy to make. The joint can be made almost indestructible by adding a couple of pegs. This is described later. For purposes of frame-and-panel joinery, a variation called the *haunched mortise-and-tenon joint* is used. This joint allows for the grooves required for the panels. The haunch on the joint is used to fill the groove on the top or bottom of the stiles. These grooves are necessary to house the inset panel. A basic mortise-and-tenon joint is shown in Illus. 4-3. A haunched mortise-and-

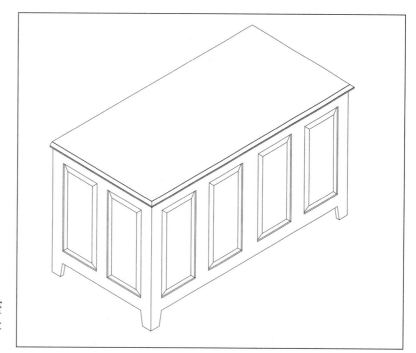

Illus. 4-1. Blanket chest with frame-and-panel carcasses.

Illus. 4-2(below). Parts of a frame-and-panel blanket chest.

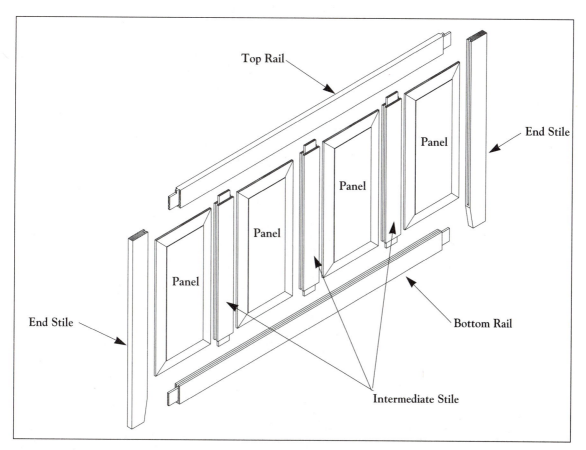

tenon joint is shown in Illus. 4-4.

The first step in making a mortise-and-tenon joint is to mark it out. The mortising gauge and square (Illus. 4-5) are used to mark out. The mortising gauge is very similar to a regular marking gauge except it has an extra pin that is movable. Set the two pins apart to match the thickness of the mortise. Then set the fence the appropriate distance from the nearest pin.

After the thickness is marked out, it's time to mark the width of the mortise. One way to

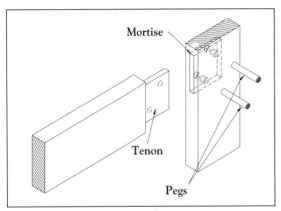

Illus. 4-3. Mortise-and-tenon joint.

ensure that the joints line up is to mark them at the same time. Illus. 4-6 shows how this is done. It's pretty easy to mess up a measurement. This is a good way to avoid that kind of error.

There is no set rule as to how long the tenon should be. When a tenon is being fit into wide boards, a couple of inches is usually adequate. If a tenon is any longer, you'll risk joining cross-grain areas within the joint. Yet, a tenon should be long enough so you can peg the joint.

Cutting the mortise can be accomplished in several ways. The traditional method is to use a mortising chisel, as shown in Illus. 4-7. Wrap a piece of tape around the chisel to mark the depth of the cut. Start about a quarter inch from one end, with the bevel of the chisel facing the end of the mortise. Hold the chisel vertically and across the grain of the stock. Drive the chisel into the stock with a mallet. Move the chisel about an eighth of an inch and drive it in again. The farther you get from the original cut, the easier it will be to drive the tool into the wood. With each cut, the wood will break out, forming the mortise cavity. Continue "chopping" this way until you are within a quarter inch of the other end. Turn the chisel around, which rotates its cut-

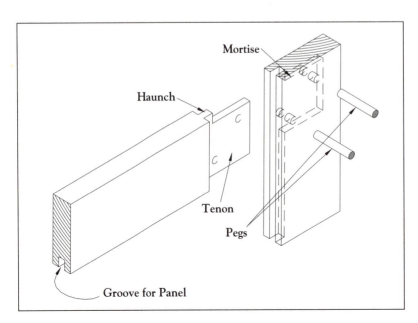

Illus. 4-4. Haunched mortise-and-tenon joint.

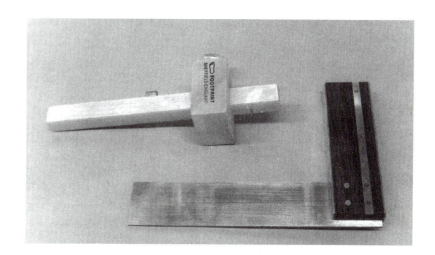

Illus. 4-5. Mortising gauge and square.

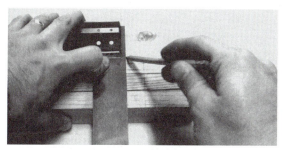

Illus. 4-6. Mark the joints at the same time, to avoid measurement errors.

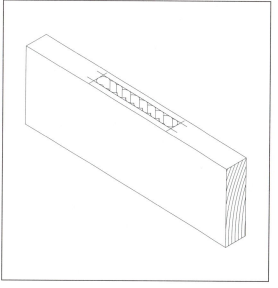

Illus. 4-8. Holes bored to start a mortise.

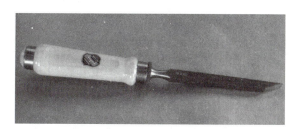

Illus. 4-7. A mortising chisel.

ting edge, and finish cutting the mortise. You'll have to go back to the start area and finish taking it to final depth. When you've finished chopping the mortise, you may want to take a regular chisel and dress up the walls and do final trimming to the layout lines.

One popular way to cut a mortise is to bore a series of holes in the edge of the board to clear the bulk of the waste (Illus. 4-8).

After the holes are bored, a chisel is used to trim to the layout lines. This method has been around for a long time. In years gone by, a brace and bit were used to bore the holes. This method is just as effective today. An updated approach would be to use a portable drill equipped with a brad-point or Forstner-type bit. Wrap the drill bits with tape to mark the depth of the mortise. Another option is to use a drill press, which would keep the holes properly aligned.

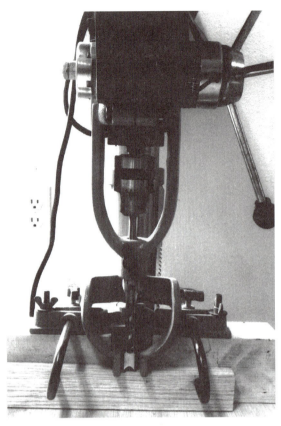

Illus. 4-9 The mortising attachment in use on a drill press.

If you do have a drill press, you might want to look into the mortising attachments that are on the market (Illus. 4-9). These are accessories that are available for most drill presses. The mortising attachment is a square, hollow chisel that is mounted on the shaft. A special drill bit turns inside the chisel. As the drill bit removes waste, the square chisel is forced into the stock, forming a square hole. The instructions for using these attachments are generally the same. Bore one square hole on one end of the mortise and make several overlapping cuts until you get to the other end.

The router can also be used to make mortises. It seems that everywhere you look you find a new jig for using the router to do various tasks. This also includes the task of making a mortise. The easiest way to make a mortise with a router is to use a router table with a fence. Several manufacturers market bits especially designed for mortising. Some look like a regular straight bit, and some have spiral flutes similar to those on a drill bit for more efficient waste removal.

To use the router table to make a mortise, draw a line on the router table fence that aligns with both the inside and outside edge of the bit you are using (Illus. 4-10). You may

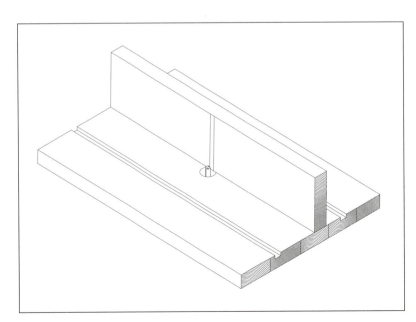

Illus. 4-10. A router table set up for mortising.

Illus. 4-11. Backsaw.

have to make multiple passes if the mortise is going to be very deep. Limit each pass to about ¼ inch. Make sure that you've marked the mortise on the edge of the stock opposite the actual mortise, so you can see the layout where it starts and stops.

Now, simply plunge the stock down onto the spinning bit and move it slowly until the layout lines align with the marks on the fence. Feed your stock from right to left and be sure to keep it against the fence.

After using a router to make a mortise, you'll have to square the ends of the mortise with a chisel. Another approach is to leave the round ends and round over the edges of the tenons. Both methods are fairly common. The choice is yours.

Cutting the tenon is a fairly straightforward operation. You can do it with a handsaw or table saw. The backsaw or tenon saw is the tool of choice when making tenons by hand. It has a reinforcement along the back edge of the blade which makes it rigid (Illus. 4-11). Start by cutting the shoulders, as shown in Illus. 4-12. These are the most critical cuts because they control the overall size of the frame. Cut the cheeks with the board held vertically in a vise.

There are some fairly simple techniques to help ensure accurate cuts when using a table saw. First, you can use a stop block attached to the rip fence to locate the shoulder cuts (Illus. 4-13). Do *not* run the end of the stock along the rip fence while pushing it with the mitre gauge! This is an invitation for stock "kickback," a situation where the stock might bind between the blade and rip fence. The result is

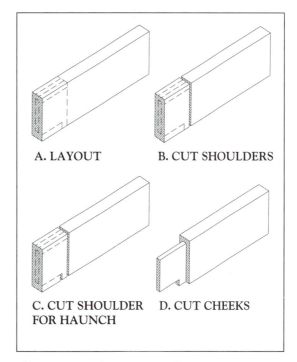

A. LAYOUT   B. CUT SHOULDERS

C. CUT SHOULDER   D. CUT CHEEKS
FOR HAUNCH

Illus. 4-12. The sequence for cutting tenons.

the blade throwing the stock in your direction with significant force. The stop block acts as a spacer between your stock and the rip fence and prevents pieces from getting "stuck" between the blade and fence. Simply bring the stock up to the block and then make your pass over the blade. Using a setup like this will ensure uniform cuts.

Cutting the cheeks on a table saw is more difficult. I've seen some people set up the rip fence and guide the stock along it. *This is not safe!* The blade guard has to be removed for

Illus. 4-13. Note the stop block attached to the rip fence, which is used to locate rip cuts.

Illus. 4-14. A tenoning jig in use.

this operation, and the hands get pretty close to the blade. Several manufacturers sell "tenoning jigs." Besides holding the stock and moving it over the blade, they keep hands at a safe distance from the blade. The tenoning jigs on the market range in price from inexpensive to outrageous.

You could build a very effective tenoning jig. Illus. 4-14 shows such a jig in use. The plans for this tenoning jig are in Chapter 19. To use it, simply raise the saw blade to the shoulder cut and adjust the saw's fence to align the layout lines of the tenon with the blade. Always set up so that the waste pieces do *not* fall in between the blade and tenoning jig or fence.

The tenon jig is used to cut the cheeks on the width of the board. It won't help for those cuts across the thickness of the stock. These are best approached with a table saw that has a sliding table with a high fence, such as that used to cut the dovetails discussed on pages 46–48. Position the tenon stock by aligning the layout marks with a slot made by passing the jig over the blade. Clamp the stock in place and push the jig over the blade.

Another method for making tenons with a table saw is to use a dado set. Illus. 4-15 shows the basic setup. It's a simple matter of installing the dado set and raising it to the

layout line on the stock. Set up your fence or mitre gauge just as you would for cutting the shoulder of the tenon. Make your first pass to cut the shoulder and follow up with multiple passes to clear the rest of the waste. There are

Illus. 4-15. A table saw with a dado set set up to make a tenon.

a couple of things to keep in mind when using this technique. First, select a dado cutter that provides the smoothest cut. Second , remember that most dado cutters leave a pretty rough surface when cutting across the grain. As we discussed in Chapter 3, the best glue joint is a tight-fitting, smooth, edge-grain-to-edge-grain joint.

Reinforcing the Joint with Pegs

On joints which are of particular structural importance, the joint can be "pegged." Using pegs (sometimes called "pinning") is the technique of boring a hole through the joint and driving a dowel in to lock the joint together. The hole is not bored completely through the joint. It usually goes through the mortised part on the "hidden" side (the side not normally in view) and passes through the tenon and partway into the wood on the other side (Illus. 4-16). A pinned mortise-and-tenon joint is *very* strong. It's a technique that's been used

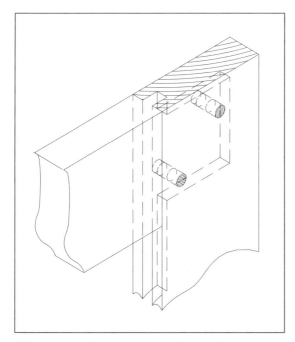

Illus. 4-16. Section view of pinned mortise-and-tenon joint.

for centuries in the construction of timber-framed buildings. You'll find these joints very useful for heavy frames such as the router table in Chapter 18. They are also effective for larger frame-and-panel furniture projects and doors such as those on the bookcase project featured throughout this book.

Don't confuse pegging a joint with the common practice of driving a small brad or nail through the joint. Many people like to do the latter to hold the joint in place while the glue cures. The advantage is that it reduces the number of clamps a person has to keep in the shop. The disadvantage is that the brad or nail will not provide structural strength. It will flex over time as the parts move with seasonal conditions and could actually break off. The nails also leave a "blemish" in the work that can be hard to conceal if the nails were put in from the visible side.

A peg, on the other hand, is a structural part of the joint. It's glued into place, so it will not break off and provides a better "lock." It may, over time, seem to work its way out slightly. This is because it's inserted across the thickness grain of the mortise-and-tenon joint. This movement is a natural occurrence and could take many years to develop, depending on the wood species and thickness of the joint. These pegs seldom move more than the thickness of a couple of sheets of paper.

Actually, the peg isn't moving. This effect occurs because parts of the joint shrink and become thinner in dry climates at a greater rate than the peg, which is inserted along the length of the grain.

There are times when the peg has to be driven in from the visible side of the joint. In such cases, it's obviously preferable to use a peg of the same species as the wood used to make the joint. Some people use square pegs. Can a square peg be put in a round hole? Yes! Cut the peg to the dimension of the hole and use a knife to whittle one end to fit. Set the peg in place and drive it in with a mallet. Take care not to drive the peg so hard as to damage the mortised frame member or to have the peg too much larger than the hole. An oversized

Illus. 4-17. A flush-cutting saw.

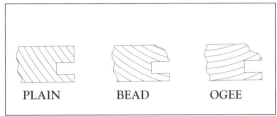

PLAIN   BEAD   OGEE

Illus. 4-18. Frame mouldings.

peg could split the frame when you drive it in. Try to orient the peg such that its top and bottom edges are horizontal when the joint is finished. If not, it could look sloppy.

Whether you use round or square pegs, leave them long and trim them flush after the glue cures. Put some glue on the end of the peg going in the hole. Don't try to glue the entire length of the peg. This isn't necessary because the glue will be spread during insertion. Wipe off any glue from around the peg with a *damp* sponge or cloth, that is, one that has been "wrung out" so it won't drip when squeezed. A wet sponge could spread the glue into the surface of the wood, causing problems when it's time to apply any stains or other finishing material later.

Some people might be tempted to trim a peg flush with the wood using a belt sander. This is not a good idea! Not only does it concentrate wear and tear on a sanding belt, there is the chance that the machine might slip and irreparably damage the surface of the wood. The best method is to cut the peg flush with an offset saw specially designed for this task. Illus. 4-17 shows a saw of this type. They are not very expensive and are designed to not mar the surface they are being used on. After the peg has been cut, dress it up by using a scraper, plane, or sanding it.

DECORATIVE TREATMENTS FOR FRAMES AND PANELS

There are many decorative treatments you can apply to the frames and the panels. Illus. 4-18 shows some examples of moulding that can be applied to the frames. The simplest is no treat-

ment at all. It is used in Shaker and old-country furniture.

These mouldings can be applied with moulding planes or scratch stocks if you prefer to work without power tools. The grooves can be made with a "plow" plane.

The old-fashion wooden moulding planes are not readily available on today's market. A lot of people wish they were. They are quicker to use than routers and shapers, which have to be set up. Furniture makers of years gone by often made their own moulding planes by shaping the bottom of the plane in reverse of the shape they wanted to cut and shaping an iron to match it. Illus. 4-19 shows a traditional moulding plane. There are some steel moulding planes on the market which have a variety of interchangeable irons. They have one major drawback: cost. They also have to be set up when you want to change shapes. It could

Illus. 4-19. Panel-raising plane. (*Photo courtesy of Garret Wade.*)

actually be less expensive in many cases to buy a good router and router bits.

Scratch stocks (Illus. 4-20) are another hand tool used to mould the edge of a board. The steel of the scratch stock is shaped by filing an old saw blade to a shape in reverse of the shape you want to produce on the wood. This blade is then held in a wooden handle and drawn along the edge of the frame member. Scratch stocks aren't especially fast tools to use, but there is no limit to the variety of patterns you can create.

Routers, shapers, and table saws used with moulding heads are the most common power tools used. There are a variety of router bit sets on the market called stile/rail sets. Besides cutting the moulding pattern, they will cut the groove for the panel in the same pass. These sets usually come with two bits (Illus. 4-21). One bit shapes the edge of the frame members. The other shapes the ends of the rails to fit the stile. This fit is sometimes referred to as "coping" (Illus. 4-22).

The home woodworker tends to cut all of the stiles and rails individually, and then shape them for assembly. Since the rail bits do leave quite a bit of tear-out, I like to cut boards to

Illus. 4-21. Stile/rail router-bit set.

length that are wide enough for three or more rails and then cut the moulding on their ends before ripping the rails to width. After all the rails are cut to size, the shaped ends are used to set the height for the stile bit, which cuts the moulding on long edges of the parts.

Stile/rail bit sets were originally meant for building projects such as kitchen or bath cabinet doors. They work quite well on such projects. When stile/rail bit sets are used, most of the glue surfaces are end grain to edge grain;

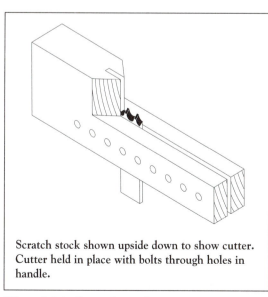

Scratch stock shown upside down to show cutter. Cutter held in place with bolts through holes in handle.

Illus. 4-20. Scratch stock.

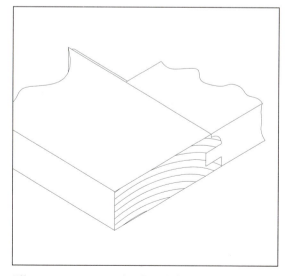

Illus. 4-22. Note the fit of the rail and stile made by stile/rail router-bit sets.

this makes the sets unsuitable for larger applications. The tenons formed by the sets are usually about ⅜ inch long. This isn't enough for pegging the joint.

There is a method in which stile/rail bit sets are used for larger carcasses. It consists of using only the stile moulding bit to shape the edges. After the edges are shaped, a tenon is cut on the ends of the rails (or intermediate members) and mortises are cut on the stiles. The moulded edges are then mitred and a section of the moulding of the stiles is removed, as shown in Illus. 4-23.

Cut the mortise in the slot made by the stile bit (Illus. 4-24). It should be at least one inch deeper than the groove. The tenons are best cut on the table saw using the tenon jig discussed earlier.

To cut the tenons, start with the shoulders. One side of the tenon will be set up by aligning the blade from the front side of the cut, and the other side of the tenon is set up by aligning the blade from the back side of the cut. This is necessary because the moulding is usually placed on one edge of the workpiece and you want to use the actual workpiece to set up the cut. The setup can be simpler when working with intermediate stiles or rails where both edges are shaped.

There are a couple of techniques for removal of waste on the mortised part of the joint. First, when the joint is on the end of the stile, the cut can be made on a table saw using a high fence on the mitre gauge just as is done when cutting tenons on the table saw (Illus. 4-25). The cut could also be made with a handsaw, but the cut must be straight and smooth to produce a tight-appearing joint on assembly. If you use a handsaw, cut slightly short of the layout line and clean the cut up with a *sharp* chisel.

Occasionally, there will be a need for a mortise-and-tenon joint that is the middle of a stile (Illus. 4-26). Removing the waste here is a bit more difficult than removing waste on the end of the stile. You could remove it using a dado set on the table saw or with a coping saw. Either way, the finished cut line will be rough. Cut close to the layout line and finish

by cleaning up with a *sharp* chisel.

After the waste moulding has been removed from a joint, it's time to cut the mitres. The easiest and cleanest mitre cuts can be made using a sharp chisel and guide block as shown in Illus. 4-27. The block is easily made (Illus. 4-28).

Using the guide block is easy. Place the

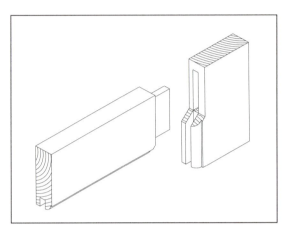

Illus. 4-23. The completed but disassembled joint.

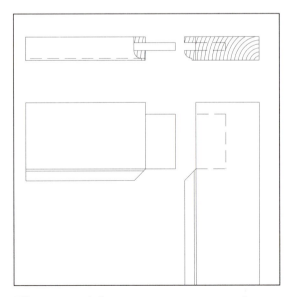

Illus. 4-24. A large-carcass mortise-and-tenon joint.

Illus. 4-25. The waste on the mortised part of a mortise-and-tenon joint can be removed on a table saw when a high fence is used on a mitre gauge.

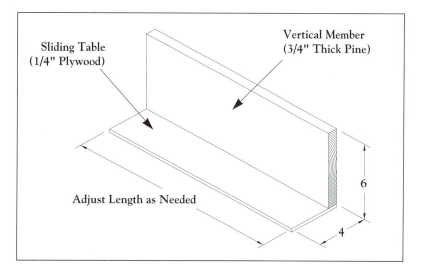

Sliding Table (1/4" Plywood)

Vertical Member (3/4" Thick Pine)

Adjust Length as Needed

6

4

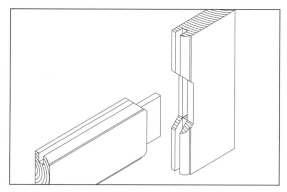

Illus. 4-26. A disassembled mid-span joint.

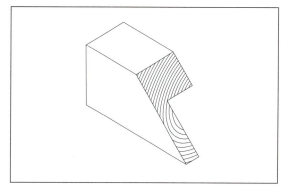

Illus. 4-28. The guide block can be easily made.

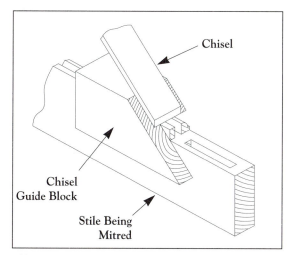

Chisel

Chisel Guide Block

Stile Being Mitred

Illus. 4-27. A guide block in use.

workpiece in a vise, set the block on the workpiece, and align the bevel of the chisel with the mitre layout line. Use the block to guide the chisel to make the cut. Use care not to drive the chisel beyond the stop line. On hard woods, make several paring cuts, working back to the mitre line. Use hand pressure only. Do not use mallets!

THE PANELS

Panels used on the frame-and-panel carcass can range from simple ¼-inch flat panels to elaborately formed raised panels. Today, the flat panels are most frequently made of plywood. Whether you are using simple or raised panels, do *not* glue them in place. They must float freely to allow for seasonal movement of the wood panel and frame.

Panels can be "raised" with a variety of profile shapes. The most common are shown in Illus. 4-29.

The table saw is often used by the home craftsman to raise a panel in a bevelled shape. The technique is fairly straightforward. For safety, a jig should be used. This jig (Illus. 4-30) is similar to the tenoning jig described on page 62. The only difference is a larger vertical panel.

Start raising the panel by making a cut around the raised portion to provide a well-defined edge (Illus. 4-31). These cuts should be about $\frac{1}{16}$ inch deep. They are usually set in about $1\frac{1}{2}$ inches from the edge of the panel. Without these cuts, the edge of the raised area wouldn't be noticeable, and the grain would be "fuzzy."

Cut the bevels by setting the table-saw blade about 5 degrees off the vertical and using the jig to move the stock over the blade. The blade should be elevated to the line formed by the earlier cuts. To get the best results, make the bevel cut in a couple of full-depth passes. The first one should be about $\frac{1}{32}$ to $\frac{1}{16}$ inch

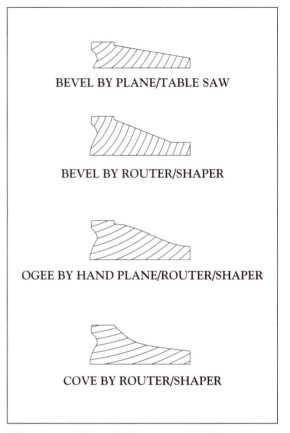

BEVEL BY PLANE/TABLE SAW

BEVEL BY ROUTER/SHAPER

OGEE BY HAND PLANE/ROUTER/SHAPER

COVE BY ROUTER/SHAPER

Illus. 4-29. Several shape options for raised panels.

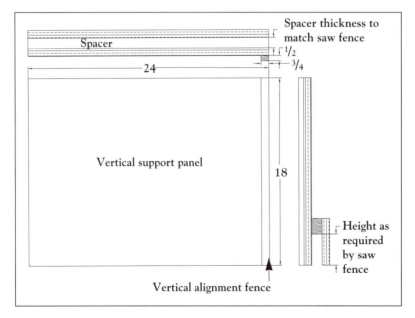

Spacer

Spacer thickness to match saw fence

$\frac{1}{2}$

$\frac{3}{4}$

24

18

Vertical support panel

Height as required by saw fence

Vertical alignment fence

Illus. 4-30. A jig used to raise panels on a table saw.

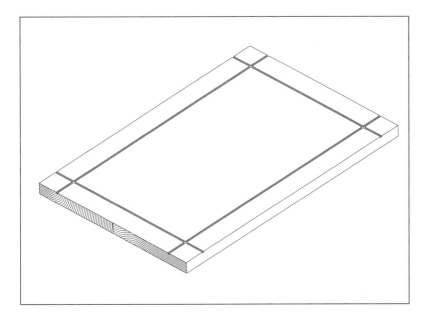

Illus. 4-31. A panel with cuts.

from the layout line, and the second should be made from the first cut to the line. The first cut will produce a fairly rough-cut surface, and the second will clean it up. Move the stock slowly while making the second pass.

This technique is quite effective when you are using ½-inch-thick stock for the panels. If you wish to use thicker stock, either raise the back surface like you did the front or form a rabbet on the back side to create the edge that will slide into the frame members (Illus. 4-32).

There are several router bits on the market for forming a raised panel. All of them require a router with at least 1½ horsepower that's capable of handling a ½-inch shank. Whether you use the conventional bits (Illus. 4-33) or the newer vertical types, there are a few points to consider. First, you will be creating a *lot* of wood dust and chips that will need to be cleaned up. You can save a lot of cleanup time by attaching a vacuum or dust collector to your router table. Always set your router up on a good router table when raising panels. Always cut mould on the end-grain edges first, so the tear-out will be cleaned up when you cut the mould on the long edges.

Raising a panel with a router involves removal of quite a bit of wood. The best plan

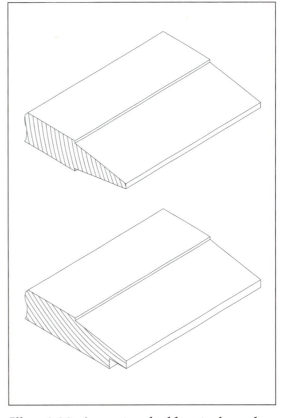

Illus. 4-32. At top is a double raised panel. Below it is a raised panel with a rabbet.

Illus. 4-33. A conventional panel-raising bit.

is to take several passes. To get the best results, make the final pass a *very* thin one. This will give you the smoothest moulding.

Many people have voiced concern about the safety of using conventional panel-raising router bits. They are worried about the large size of the bit and the stresses placed on it when it's working. These bits have been in use for quite some time and I have not heard of any problems other than those that happen when ordinary router safety warnings are ignored.

Conventional panel-raising bits have one advantage over the vertical bits: They can work on a curved panel, while vertical bits are limited to straight edges. When using such a large router bit, you get significantly improved results if you can slow your router speed down to around 11,000 RPM. There are speed controllers available on the market and a new breed of variable-speed routers that can handle the job.

Panels can also be raised on a shaper. The shaper is essentially a heavy-duty version of a router mounted in a router table. Shapers can cut a wider variety of shapes and operate at slower speeds than routers. They also cost several times more than a good router; a shaper is a machine most beginning woodworkers cannot afford.

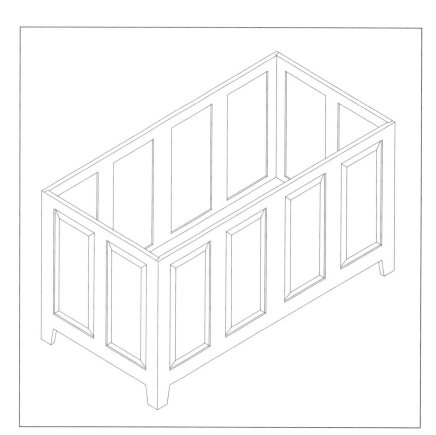

Illus. 4-34. The assembled carcass of a blanket chest.

ASSEMBLING THE CARCASS

After the panels and frames are assembled, it's time to join these parts to form the carcass (Illus. 4-34). The joinery used is straightforward. You could use simple edge-glued, tongue-and-groove, mitre, or rabbet joints (Illus. 4-35).

The simple edge-glued joint is very strong. However, when an edge-glued joint on larger projects is being glued up, it may be difficult to keep its parts aligned. In these instances, a tongue-and-groove, edge-glued joint would be better.

A rabbet joint provides a couple of advantages over a basic edge-glue joint. It provides more glue area and its parts are easier to keep aligned during glue-up. Another advantage of the rabbet joint is that it will hide dadoes you may use to install the bottom.

A mitre joint could also be used, but because these joints don't interlock they are difficult to work with when assembling the carcass. The solution is a modification called

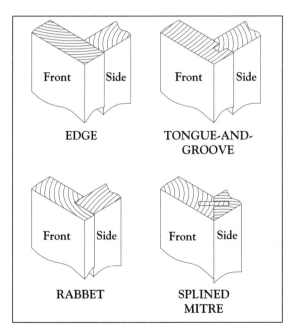

Illus. 4-35. A variety of joints that can be used to assemble the carcass.

the *splined mitre joint*. Simply cut a slot or groove and a spline to fit the grooves, as shown in Illus. 4-35. These operations are best accomplished on a table saw.

Do *not* use dovetail joints! Edge-grain dovetails are not very strong. In fact, any twist could easily break off the tails and pins, because the wood would simply split along the grain.

When the fronts, backs, and sides of a frame-and-panel carcass are assembled, they are seldom flush with smooth-fitting joints. This is why the parts are usually cut a little "long" for final trimming. It's easier to trim a little off the end of the front or back than to trim the sides to match them. The best way to do this is with a plane.

Some people might be tempted to trim the parts with a belt sander. Unless you are well experienced with these machines, it isn't a very good idea. A belt sander will tend to round over the wood and eliminate that crisp corner. Sure, the corner may be shaped anyway, but the belt sander will make the corner "out of square."

There are essentially three methods for installing bottoms in raised panel carcasses. In all cases, it's important to *not* glue the bottom to the carcass. Remember, the wood has to "float," to allow for seasonal movement.

One method has already been discussed. Form a groove or dado along the lower rails of the frames and insert a panel (Illus. 4-36). The panel could be a simple sheet of plywood or several boards. A second method is to attach some cleats as shown in Illus. 4-37. You could lay the bottom on these cleats and fasten it in place through slotted holes.

Using a base frame (discussed later) will also give you a place to insert a bottom by laying the panel on top of the frame (Illus. 4-38).

Any time panels are cut to fit into a glued-up carcass, there will be a few gaps in a carcass. You may wish to cover these with some decorative moulding. This moulding should be glued/nailed *only* to the lower rail of the frame-and-panel, not to the bottom panel. Regardless of the type of bottom you install, make sure to cut it to leave some room for sea-

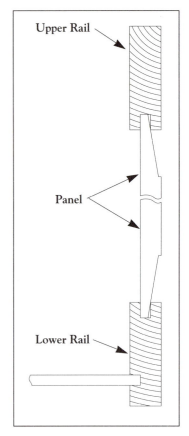

Illus. 4-36. The bottom panel inserted into dadoes.

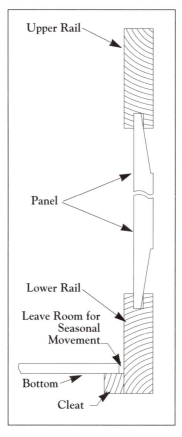

Illus. 4-37. A view of the batten or cleat on the lower rail.

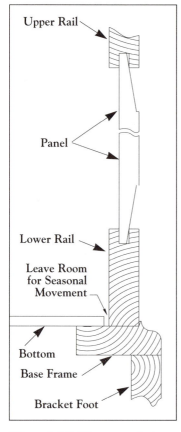

Illus. 4-38. You can also install bottoms in raised-panel carcasses by using a base frame.

sonal movement. Solid-wood panels will move a lot more than plywood.

When a chest such as the one illustrated in this chapter is used to store blankets, quilts, or other needlework, it's a common practice to use aromatic cedar for the bottom. This is a traditional, and effective, way to prevent insect damage. A common approach is to use a thin plywood bottom and put a lining of closet lining cedar over it. You can get this cedar at most lumber stores. A solid cedar bottom could be made up to fit in a dado. A solid cedar bottom could be produced by inserting cedar boards with lapped or tongue-and-groove joints in a grooved frame. The strips of cedar are *not* glued together, to allow for seasonal movement. ◨

5 INTERNAL FRAMES

The internal frame (Illus. 5-1) is a relatively simple assembly composed of front, back, and end rails. The front rail is usually visible and, as such, is generally made of the same primary wood as the carcass. The side and end rails, on the other hand, are generally made of less-expensive secondary wood such as pine or poplar. When used to support drawers, special intermediate rails running from front to back are often used as drawer guides. These rails work by providing a means for the drawer side to slide along, by fitting in the notches cut in the backs of drawers, or by providing a way to support some of the plastic drawer guides which are on the market (Illus. 5-2).

The frames are usually built using either mortise-and-tenon or tongue-and-groove joints (Illus. 5-3). Whichever you select, remember that the side rails and any intermediate rails running from front to back are what directly support the drawers. It's important to get a good mechanical engagement between these and the front and rear members of the frame.

There are some decisions to be made when building the frames. Cross-grain joinery problems can occur when the side rails of a frame are attached to the carcass side. This can be addressed during frame construction *and/or* during installation. In either case, the frame sides must *not* be glued along the entire width of the carcass side.

Some people prefer not to glue the side rails to the front and end rails, choosing instead to glue the front and end rails in place in the carcass and allow the side rails to "float," loosely supported at the front and end. When tongue-and-groove construction is used to build the frame, and simple dadoes used to install the frame, fix the end rail in place with a *single* screw halfway back. To avoid any cross-grain joinery problems, be sure to make the side rails somewhat short ($1/4$ inch), to allow for seasonal movement of the side panels. With the front and back frame rails glued to the carcass side, they will move relative to the "floating" end rails.

The other option is to glue the frames to form an assembly. When installing a glued-up frame, apply glue only on the front two or three inches, to allow the rest of the end panels of the carcass to move relative to the

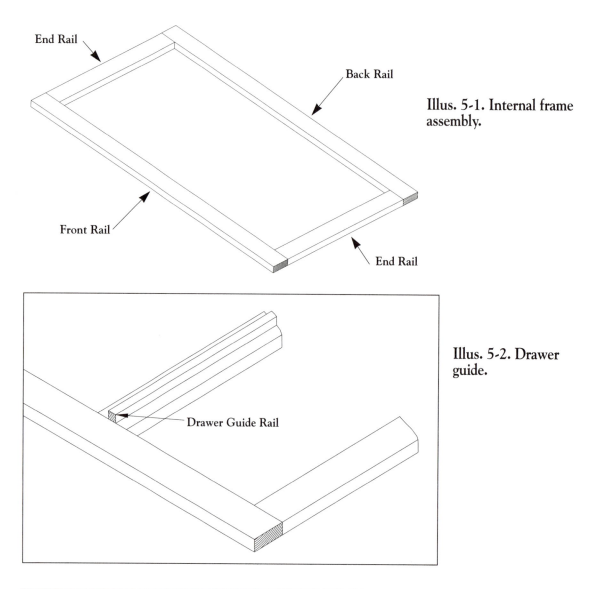

Illus. 5-1. Internal frame assembly.

Illus. 5-2. Drawer guide.

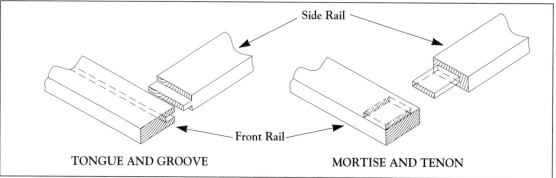

TONGUE AND GROOVE   MORTISE AND TENON

Illus. 5-3. Mortise-and-tenon and tongue-and-groove joints are usually used to build frames.

frames. Be sure you glue the front. If you glue the back, the end panel will move relative to the frame, and they will not appear to "fit" together.

By far, the two most popular joinery methods for installing the drawer frames are the dado and the sliding dovetail (Illus. 5-4). Each is discussed below.

THE DADO JOINT

The dado joint is the easier of the two joints to make. When considering the dado, remember the glue joints will be end grain to long grain. Don't rely on them to tie the sides of the carcass together structurally. Depending on the size of the carcass, this may not be a problem. The joint can be made using a variety of methods.

The full-thickness dado joint has two drawbacks. First, there is no shoulder to pro-

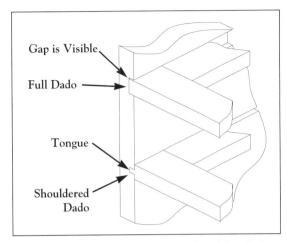

Illus. 5-5. Full thickness and shoulder dado joints. If the full-thickness dado joint is too wide, the gap will be visible all along the top of the frame.

vide more stability. Second, if the dado is too wide by *any* amount, or the frame member is not level and flat, a gap will be visible where the frame meets the carcass side. This is shown in Illus. 5-5. Any gap on the shouldered joint would only be visible on the end of the joint, which is often covered by a face frame.

Cutting the Dado by Hand

Lay out the dado and be sure to mark the depth of the cut on both edges of the board. Cut a kerf with a handsaw. Be sure to keep the kerf on the inside of the layout line, as shown in Illus. 5-6. Saw the kerf to the layout lines on the edges of the side. A board could be clamped along the layout line to guide the saw and keep the cut straight.

After the edges of the dado are defined by the saw kerfs, the waste is removed with a chisel. A hammer or mallet is not needed here. Push the chisel gently into the wood. Don't go all the way to the bottom of the dado at this stage. Simply remove the bulk of the material and later smooth the bottom with a sharp chisel (Illus. 5-7).

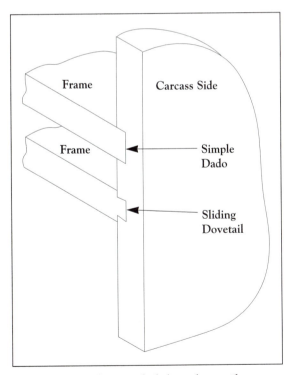

Illus. 5-4. Dadoes and sliding dovetails are the two joints most often used to install drawer frames.

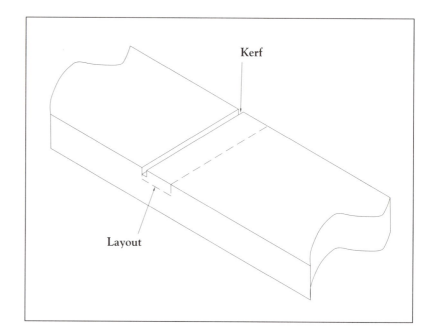

Illus. 5-6. Cut the kerf on the inside of the layout line.

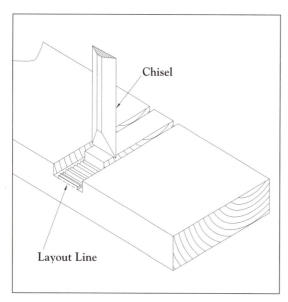

Illus. 5-7. Use a chisel to remove the dado waste.

Cutting the Dado by Machine

Dadoes can also be cut using either a dado set on a table saw or a router table. If you use the router table, either make the panel wider than the width needed or attach scrap pieces to prevent the router from making a mess of the entry and exit holes on the board. Since we are cutting across the grain of carcass side panels, the table saw's mitre gauge will be used to feed the stock over the cutter. The various types of dado cutters were discussed in Chapter 3.

Aligning the wood to locate the cut can be a challenge (Illus. 5-8). There is a quick trick to make sure the dado is placed where you want it. Start by making your layout line on the side of the stock *opposite* where you want the dado cut. Make an attachment for the mitre gauge similar to the one used for dovetails on the table saw (pages 46–48). The sliding table will probably need to be widened to work with wider stock. Install the dado set on the saw and raise it to about ¼ inch higher than the stock thickness. Pass the mitre gauge with the wooden fence over the dado set. Reset the height of the dado set to the layout line on the edge of the board. Now, all you have to do is align the layout lines on the outside side panels with the cut in the wood. One caution: Any time the fence is removed and put back on the mitre gauge, make sure the "guide cut" is aligned with the dado set.

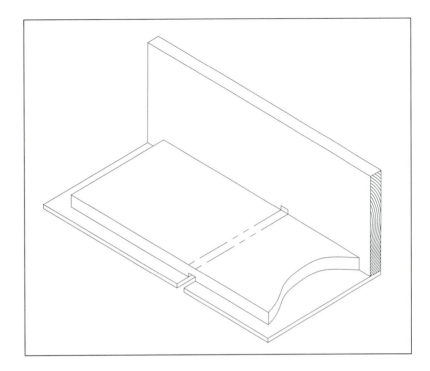

Illus. 5-8. The stock is lined up for a dado cut.

Dadoes can also be cut with a router (Illus. 5-9). The simplest method for doing this would be to clamp a *straight* board across the stock at a distance of one half the diameter of the router base from the centerline of the dado (Illus. 5-10).

Both side panels need to be cut. Depending on the width of the sides, you may want to glue up a single panel, which you can later rip to yield both panels after the dadoes have been cut. Or, you could clamp the sides together while cutting the dadoes with a router. In either case, the purpose is to get the dadoes aligned precisely when the carcass is assembled. Obviously, working with a single panel would give the best level of control. Sometimes, as in a tool chest, the same consideration applies to cutting dadoes to support vertical drawer dividers.

The standard dado joint is visible when there is no face frame on the carcass. There may be times when you prefer not to see the joint, in which case a *stopped dado* should be used (Illus. 5-11).

The stopped dado joint is a simple derivative of the standard dado. As shown in Illus.

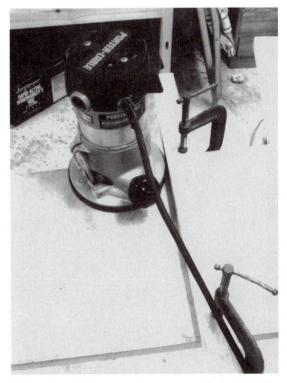

Illus. 5-9. The setup for cutting dadoes with a router.

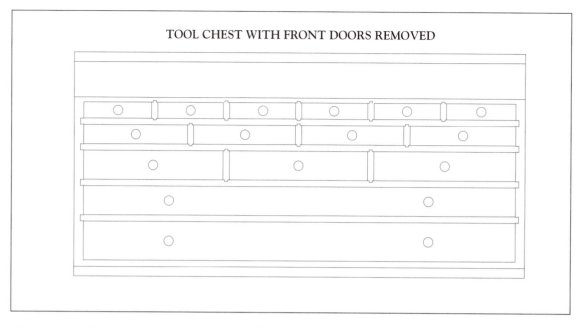

TOOL CHEST WITH FRONT DOORS REMOVED

Illus. 5-10. Note the drawer divider installation in this tool chest.

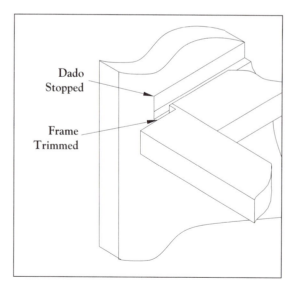

Dado
Stopped

Frame
Trimmed

Illus. 5-11. A stopped dado joint.

5-11, the dado is "stopped" short of going the full width of the board, and the frame is cut to fit the offset. This cut can be made with a handsaw. Be careful to keep the cut as square as possible. Keeping the shoulder as close to the front of the carcass as possible will help to keep the cut square.

SLIDING DOVETAIL JOINTS

Sliding dovetail joints are similar to dado joints, with one major difference. The dovetail forms an interlock between the two mating parts. The joint adds structural strength, and some people like it aesthetically. A frame installed with sliding dovetails provides a structural connection between the sides of the carcass. This is not true with a dado joint.

The best way to make a sliding dovetail joint is with the router. It could be accomplished with hand methods, but these are very tedious and require the building of a special saw for cutting the "slot."

There is a router jig on the market which can make the sliding dovetail joint. This is the most expensive of the jigs on the market, but the extra cost often yields extra capability.

A table-mounted router could also be used to make the joint.

Before making *any* cuts, mark them out

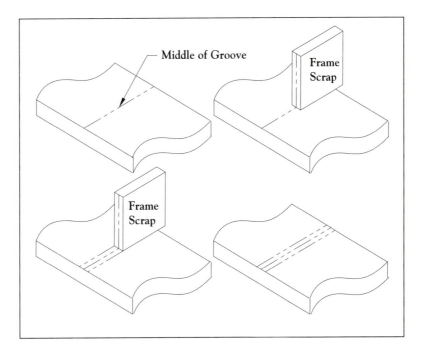

Illus. 5-12. Marking out the cuts for the sliding dovetail joint.

Middle of Groove

Frame Scrap

Frame Scrap

(Illus. 5-12). Start with the centerline of the slot. Mark the middle of the edge of a piece of scrap that's the same thickness as your frame. Set the scrap on the side panel with the centerlines aligned. Mark the thickness of the frame stock on the side panel stock.

Start by cutting the slot across the side panels. You could either cut the slot on the router table in a fashion similar to making a crosscut on a table saw, or by guiding the router across the stock with a straight board clamped to the stock. This technique would be identical to setting up for a regular dado. As the router bit enters and exits the stock, there will be some tear-out. You can minimize or eliminate this by clamping a piece of scrap on both ends of the cut. Another solution would be to cut the grooves before the sides are cut down to their final width; just leave enough width to trim about $\frac{1}{8}$ or $\frac{1}{4}$ inch off both edges.

After the slots are cut, it's time to cut the dovetail. Illus. 5-13 shows the sequence. Mount the router on the router table and raise the bit to match the depth of the slot. This is a critical adjustment which could be avoided

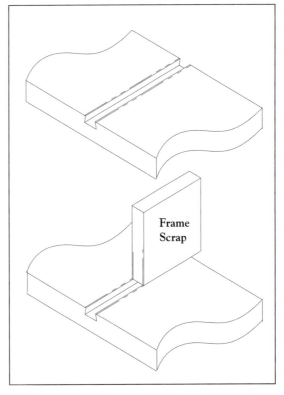

Frame Scrap

Illus. 5-13. The sequence for making a sliding dovetail joint.

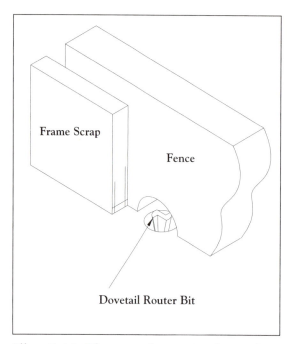

Frame Scrap

Fence

Dovetail Router Bit

Illus. 5-14. The setup for cutting dovetails with a router mounted in a router table.

by cutting the slot with the router mounted in the table.

The next adjustment will set the width of the dovetail. Set the frame-stock scrap back on the grooved board and make sure it is aligned with the marks you made earlier for the thickness of the frame. Now, mark the edge of the frame stock to align it with the width of the groove on the surface of the grooved board/panel. These marks will be used to set the fence on the router table (Illus. 5-14). Count on making several trial cuts on scrap to get the fit "just right."

The direct measurement marking used here is intended to reduce errors in transferring measurements. The joint must fit tightly and, therefore, the adjustments will be critical. ◨

6 FACE FRAME

Illus. 6-1 shows a simple kitchen base cabinet. A face frame is visible on its front. Face frames are made of horizontal rails and vertical stiles. Often, as on this cabinet, intermediate stiles and rails are added to separate the carcass into various compartments. The frames will also add strength.

When the face frame is built after the carcass is completed, it is absolutely critical to get the face frame members to align with the carcass components. If such is the case with your project, use the actual carcass to mark out joint locations and other dimensions.

The joinery used on face frames is fairly simple. Most basic face frames are assembled using the lap joint (Illus. 6-2). On larger carcasses where the face frame is relied on as a structural element, mortise-and-tenon joints may be a better choice. On such "heavy-duty" face frames, you might use a combination of mortise-and-tenon joint for the primary frame and lap joints for intermediate stiles and rails. The lap joint can be made using the same techniques used for cutting dadoes. Cut the saw kerfs by hand and chisel out the waste;

then use a router or a dado cutter in a table saw to cut the joint. One critical point is to keep the joint as smooth as possible to achieve the best glue joint at assembly time. You don't have to use a dado cutter on the table saw. You could use a standard carbide-tipped blade and make the cut in several passes.

One problem that commonly occurs is not getting the cuts at exactly the correct depth. When this happens, the joint produced is not very smooth and flush (Illus. 6-3). This is easy to avoid. Start by cutting either the stiles or rails first. Do not cut both parts without using the finished parts to mark the matching parts for depth of cut. If you're using a table saw, turn the completed piece upside down and raise the dado cutter to the thickness of the stock you need to remove to make a match.

Look at Illus. 6-1 for a minute. It's obvious that the lap joints cut across the rails must line up precisely. This is not a problem. Cut the dadoes across the lumber *before* ripping it to final width (Illus. 6-4). This also applies to the stiles. To get the absolute best fit between a

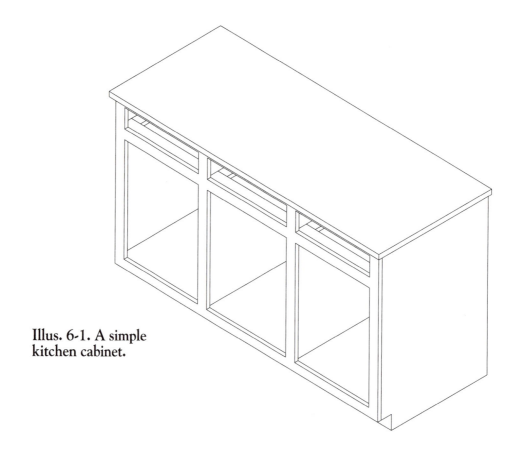

Illus. 6-1. A simple
kitchen cabinet.

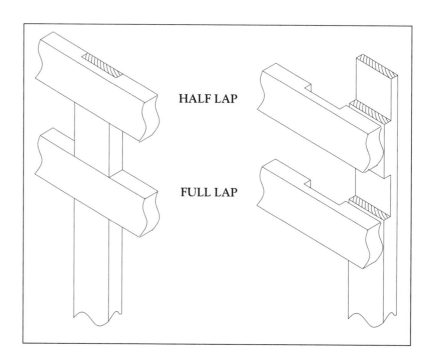

Illus. 6-2. Lap joints.

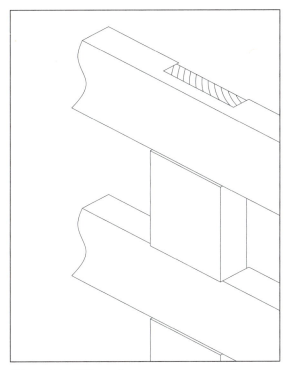

Illus. 6-3. When the cuts are not made at the correct depth, the joints on the face frame will be mismatched.

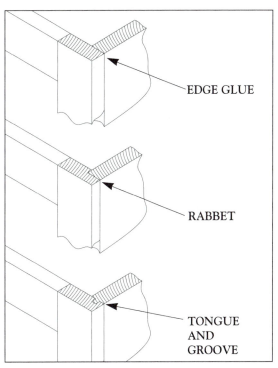

EDGE GLUE

RABBET

TONGUE
AND
GROOVE

Illus. 6-5. Basic edge glue, rabbet, or tongue-and-groove joints are used to attach the face frame to the carcass.

Illus. 6-4. Cut the dadoes across the lumber (top) before ripping it to its final width (below).

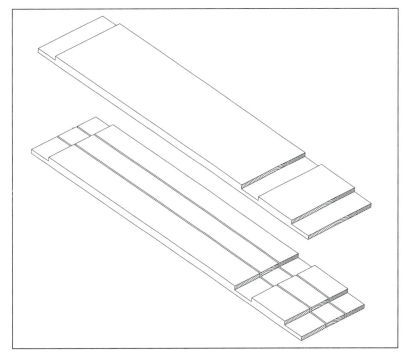
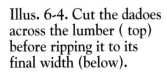

stile and a rail, rip the pieces slightly wider than needed and trim them with a hand plane. When using the hand plane, make very fine shavings and check the fit of the pieces after each pass with the plane.

Attaching the face frame to the carcass is straightforward. You can use either a basic edge-glue, rabbet, or tongue-and-groove joint (Illus. 6-5). The tongue-and-groove joint is commonly used when the carcass is made from plywood, because the edge of plywood is a poor surface for glue joints. Rabbet joints have the advantage of being easier to make when the face frame is being attached to the carcass.

Regardless of your joint selection, build your face frames so they stand slightly larger than the carcass. This will allow you to bring the face frame flush with the carcass sides by simply trimming the edge of the stiles; there is no need to sand, plane, or scrape the carcass sides. This trimming can be done with a plane or a flush-trimming bit installed in a router. Avoid the temptation to use a belt sander. If the sides of the carcass are plywood, a slip with a belt sander will quickly cut right through the outer veneer. ◨

7 CARCASS BACKS

The back of the carcass (Illus. 7-1) is overlooked as a major element in many furniture designs. It should be a major consideration, especially when the carcass is large and does not use a face frame. When a carcass back or face frame is not used, although the carcass sides or top and bottom may remain parallel to each other, the sides sometimes are not square, or perpendicular, to the top and bottom (Illus. 7-2). This is called "racking." To test a cabinet for square, measure across diagonal corners. If they are the same, the cabinet is square.

There are essentially two types of backs used: hardwood veneered plywood or several built-up, narrow boards. The grain on the top and bottom of carcasses lies perpendicular to the visible grain of the back. This makes the use of a solid, glued-up panel a poor choice except on very small cabinets.

A plywood back is easier to make than several built-up boards. A plywood back is set into a rabbet. Illus. 7-3 shows a section of the lower carcass used on the bookcase project described throughout this book. Notice how the back is inset.

When installing a plywood back, remember it will not match the seasonal movement of the other parts of the carcass. With that in mind, do *not* glue around the full edge of the plywood back. Apply the glue to approximately 2 inches of the middle of each edge. Use small nails on about 4-inch centers around the periphery. Cut the plywood slightly *short*, to allow for seasonal movement of the carcass. While not "locking" the back in place relative to the carcass, the glue and nails will keep it attached and act as a "shear panel" to prevent racking.

Besides being the easiest and quickest material to make a back from, hardwood veneered plywood is also, often, the least expensive. One-quarter-inch-thick plywood is the standard back material. An important consideration is the typical "good" and "bad" sides of the plywood. This usually restricts plywood for use on project backs that face walls.

Another look at the bookcase project in Illus. 7-1 reveals that two different types of back are being used on the upper and lower carcasses. A plywood panel was used on the bottom carcass because it is not visible. The upper carcass, on the other hand, is visible

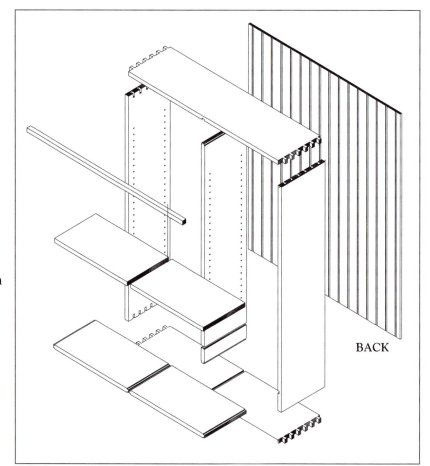

Illus. 7-1. The basic back of a carcass should also be considered a major element in furniture design.

BACK

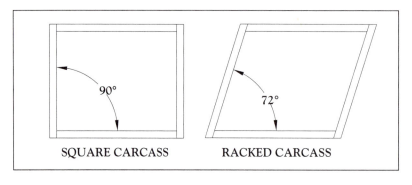

90°

72°

SQUARE CARCASS   RACKED CARCASS

Illus. 7-2. Sometimes the sides on a carcass are not square, or perpendicular, to the top and bottom.

behind the glass doors and calls for a different approach. Sure, you could use an external plywood veneer that's the same species as the carcass, but the plan calls for a more traditional approach.

The vertical lines in Illus. 7-1 represent the moulding used on the backing boards. Illus. 7-4 shows how these boards are assembled to form the "panel." This view is as seen from inside the carcass. Notice how the boards overlap each other. These moulded boards are really used in more formal settings. A back could

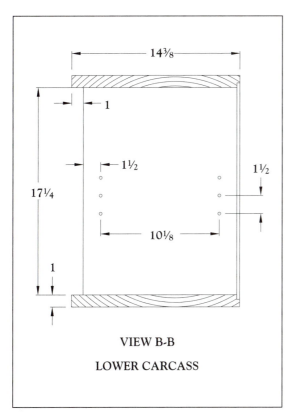

VIEW B-B

LOWER CARCASS

Illus. 7-3. A section of the lower carcass on the bookcase.

also be built up of boards without the bead moulding in less formal situations. In fact, the lower carcass of our bookcase would do quite well with a basic back of several boards of secondary wood without the beading moulding. The boards should still be "lapped" so they will support each other. This would satisfy the purists out there who don't like plywood or particleboard. (That's okay. I'm one. It's merely a matter of personal preference.)

The moulding of the backing boards can be done by hand with moulding planes or a scratch stock. It can also be accomplished with a router or a moulding head attachment used on table saws. Illus. 7-5 shows such a moulding head. You'll notice there are several cutter options.

Use wood about ⅜ inch thick for the backing boards. That will give you enough thickness for any moulding you want to cut and ensure that the board is strong enough.

Illus. 7-5. A moulding head on a table saw can be used to cut moulding on the backing boards of carcass backs. (*Photo courtesy of Delta Machinery Tool Company.*)

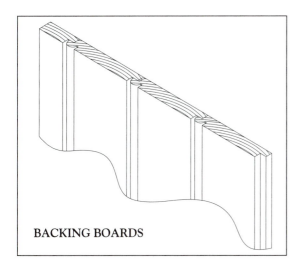

BACKING BOARDS

Illus. 7-4. The top of a built-up back, as seen from inside the carcass.

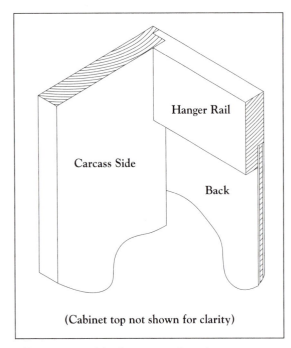

Hanger Rail

Carcass Side

Back

(Cabinet top not shown for clarity)

Illus. 7-6. Add a hanger rail to the carcass back of a wall-hung display cabinet, to provide structural strength for hanging hardware.

These backs are installed with a single nail at the top and bottom of the carcass. If there are any fixed shelves or frames, you could also put a nail there. A little glue in the middle of the backing board would also be okay, but do *not* spread it across the full width. Remember to avoid cross-grain situations. Consequently, three inches should be the maximum width of a backing board. Nails could also be spaced about 4-6 inches apart along the length of the board that overlaps the carcass side.

Although you could do a little math and divide the area covered by the back into equal spaces for a uniform board width, there is an easier way. Start by laying the middle backing board in place (do not use glue or nails now). Then work out to both edges of the carcass, installing all of the backing boards. Mark the last board to fit the final space and trim it to size. Mark the boards with numbers from one side of the carcass to the other, so they will be installed in the same order.

If your project is a wall-hung curio/display cabinet, a plywood or built-up back will not provide the structural base strength for hanging hardware, so a *hanger* rail (Illus. 7-6) should be added. The hanger rail is a strip of solid hardwood capable of taking a screw or other fastener that will support the weight of the cabinet. Its ends and top are rabbeted to fit in the rabbets of the top and sides of the carcass. The back of the rail is rabbeted to accept the back of the cabinet. ◘

8 BASE FRAME

Base frames raise the carcass up from the floor. They generally take one of two forms. The one used in the bookcase project (Illus. 8-1) has all horizontal members and bracket feet. It's a bit more "substantial" and is the type found on heavier furniture projects.

Illus. 8-2 shows a cross section of the base frame used for the bookcase. Notice that the frame has moulding and is rabbeted, to ensure a tight fit with the carcass. The moulding should be cut first. The rabbet can be made easily on a table saw. Just raise the blade to the width of the rabbet ($1\frac{7}{8}$ inches) and set your fence the thickness of the stock minus $\frac{1}{8}$ inch. Now, pass the stock along the fence vertically. Be sure to use feather boards to hold the stock against the saw fence, and a push stick to keep your hands well away from the blade.

After the stock has been formed, it is time to begin assembly of the frame. Wait until the mating carcass is finished before building the frame. For the best fit, mark the frame members directly from the carcass.

As you can see from Illus. 8-1, the front of the frame uses a mitre joint, and the back uses a tongue-and-groove joint. You can reinforce the mitre joints by gluing a piece of stock in the grooved mitre (Illus. 8-3). This will provide for some edge-grain-to-edge-grain glue joints, which are much stronger than simple mitre joints.

Some base frames are built using vertical boards (Illus. 8-4). These generally have their front/side rails and feet cut out of a single board. They are commonly used in Shaker furniture. Sometimes, the design calls for a wide moulding along the top of the base frame. If the stock thickness will not allow for the moulding *and* the rabbet, you could simply add a cleat (Illus. 8-5). Just like the horizontal frame, the front corners are put together with mitre joints. Because of the thickness of the parts, reinforcement of the joint is especially important. Glue blocks are the most common method. For larger projects, use the reinforcement braces that are screwed in place.

There will be times when you will not want any feet on the base frame. This could be a design preference or because the carcass is very large. The solution is a vertical member base frame with solid-board rails. The only difference between this base frame and the one just discussed is the width of the boards.

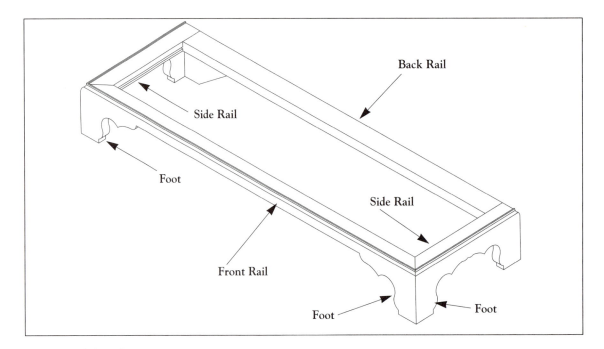

Illus. 8-1(above). Base-frame assembly for the bookcase project. Note the horizontal members and bracket feet.

Illus. 8-2. Base frame cross section.

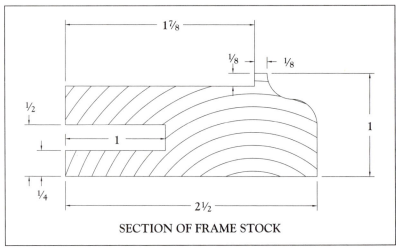

SECTION OF FRAME STOCK

The backs of side members are usually tied together structurally with a board of secondary wood (Illus. 8-6). It is as wide as the rabbet is high, to support the carcass.

When using the base frame made of horizontal members, make its bracket feet separately and glue them in place after the frame is assembled. There are times when a similar process is also better for the vertical base frame. This is especially true with complex foot designs.

Bracket feet (Illus. 8-7) can take several forms. The bow saw is the hand tool of choice for making these shapes (Illus. 8-8). They can also be cut with a sabre saw or band saw. A frequently used technique when using a band saw is to stack several boards with double-backed tape and cut them all at the same time. This will save time and ensure that all of the feet are identical. Obviously, if they are cut by hand or individually, you should expect

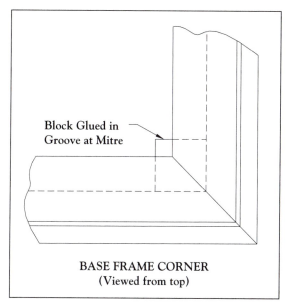

Block Glued in
Groove at Mitre

BASE FRAME CORNER
(Viewed from top)

Illus. 8-3. You can reinforce the mitre joints in the base frame by gluing a piece of stock in their grooves.

some minor variances. Usually, they won't be noticeable. Of highest priority is to make sure they are of equal height.

There are a couple of methods for attaching the base frames to the carcass. The first method consists of simply screwing the frame in place. Be careful to use slotted holes in the frame along the sides, to allow for seasonal movement. Screw through the cleat. Remember to *not* glue along the full length of the side frame member. It's okay to glue along the front only.

You could also use the traditional tabletop fastener (Illus. 8-9). These are simple devices you can make. If you make your own, make sure that the grain of the wood is perpendicular to the frame stock. Otherwise, the fastener will break easily. Several companies make similar items out of formed metal. The groove needed for these fasteners is already cut into the horizontal frame. You

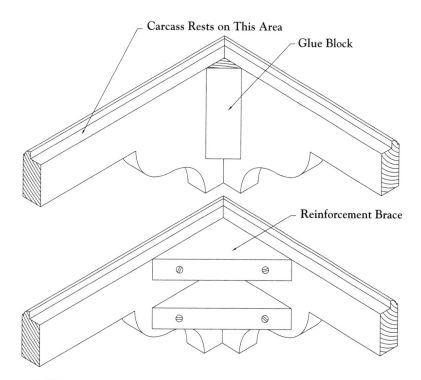

Carcass Rests on This Area

Glue Block

Illus. 8-4. Reinforcing mitre joints on vertical-board base frames.

Reinforcement Brace

INTERNAL VIEW OF VERTICAL BASE FRAME MITRE JOINT

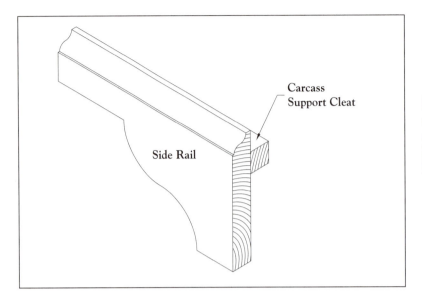

Illus. 8-5. If the design calls for a moulding and a rabbet, you sometimes have to add a cleat to the base frame.

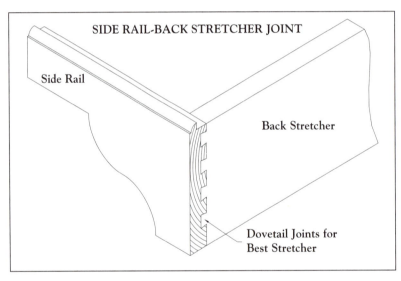

Illus. 8-6. A board is used on base frames to tie side members together structurally.

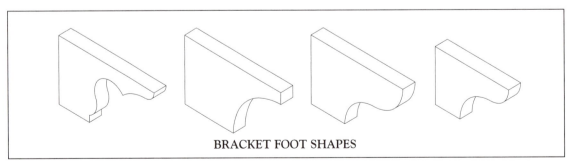

Illus. 8-7. Several bracket foot shapes.

Illus. 8-8. The bow saw is the hand tool used to shape bracket feet.

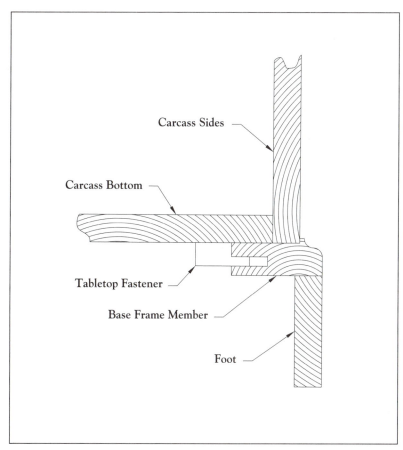

Carcass Sides

Carcass Bottom

Tabletop Fastener

Base Frame Member

Foot

Illus. 8-9. Tabletop fasteners can be used to attach base frames to carcasses.

would have to cut it into the vertical frame members.

There may be times when you want to put some feet on a project, but no frame.

There is no rule that says the frame has to be used. The bracket feet can be attached directly to the carcass. Just be careful regarding cross-grain joinery. ◘

9 ENTABLATURE

One of the biggest design issues has to do with those finishing touches that ultimately define the character of a piece of furniture. On taller pieces, like our bookcase (Illus. 9-1), the top of the cabinet is not usually used as a place to store or display anything. The stylistic design of this project calls for a pediment. This is a board set vertically on top as a design element. It has no structural function. Pediments are usually used on cabinets whose tops are above eye level. Illus. 9-2 shows a close-up of a pediment on a bookcase.

Often, the pediment board is attached to a frame, as in our project. The frame is then mounted on the top of the cabinet. It's essentially a base frame turned upside down. This arrangement allows the carcass to be assembled with the half-blind dovetail joint and allows for a decorative overhang at the top of the cabinet.

Cornices are added for decorative transition around the top of many furniture pieces. Illus. 9-3 shows a typical cornice cross section. Notice how a cornice requires the top of the carcass to overhang the side. This will influence your selection of joinery when building the carcass. You should consider using a stopped dado or stopped sliding dovetail to

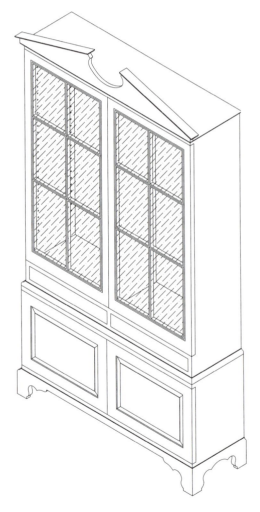

Illus. 9-1. Note the pediment on this bookcase. The pediment has no structural function. It simply acts as a design element.

94

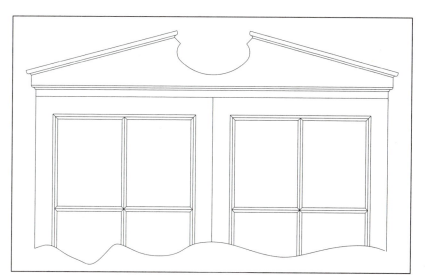

Illus. 9-2. A close-up of
the pediment.

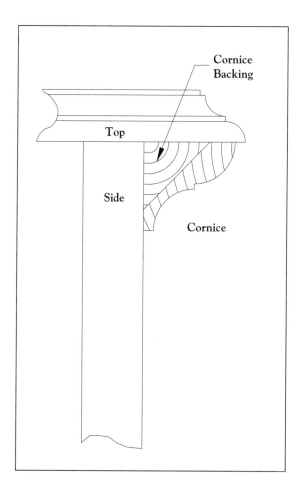

Illus. 9-3. A cross-section view of cornice.

join the sides to the top. If a dado is selected, remember there will be no mechanical interlock holding the top to the side if someone were to try to lift the cabinet by grabbing the top. This problem can be solved by using the tabletop fasteners discussed in Chapter 8. These fasteners will also help keep the top panel from cupping or warping with time.

The cornice presents another challenge. The cornice board is installed on the carcass ends so that it is across the grain of the carcass side and top. Although you could glue the cornice moulding in place on the front of a conventional carcass, do *not* glue it on its sides. If the sides are of frame-and-panel construction, the cornice moulding could be glued to the frame; avoid getting glue on the carcass top.

Illus. 9-3 shows how blocks are often used to mount cornice moulding. Sometimes these pieces run the entire width of the carcass side. Sometimes they are simply blocks spaced a few inches apart. Either way, these cornice moulding backing blocks or strips can be screwed to the carcass using slotted holes (to allow for seasonal movement); they should *not* be glued in place. The exception to this rule is to glue them at the front of the carcass side to keep the mitre joint between the side and front mouldings snug. After the backing blocks are mounted, the cornice can be glued directly to them. ◘

10 SHELVES AND PARTITIONS

Shelves take many forms (Illus. 10-1). If they are made of solid hardwood, they are glued up as any other panel. Using solid hardwood for shelving does significantly increase the amount of lumber required to build a project and, with it cost. So, many people choose to use plywood. If anything other than solid lumber is used, we'll have to strengthen the shelf if it spans any significant distance and add some hardwood to hide the edge of the stock.

Shelves can be installed permanently or made adjustable. Our bookcase uses a permanently installed shelf to act as the bottom of the upper bookcase section above the drawers. The fixed shelves are installed just like the drawer support frames discussed earlier. The only difference is solid-wood shelves do not present the cross-grain joinery problem relative to the carcass sides that the drawer support frames do. Although a solid-wood shelf will move with the carcass sides throughout the seasons, glue will not. For this reason, apply glue to no more than a couple of inches at the *front* of the carcass. This will ensure that the shelf won't "wander" out of position.

Suitable joints for attaching shelves to the carcass include the shouldered dado and sliding dovetail joints. If you're using plywood, the sliding dovetail joint really shouldn't be used. Plywood must be given the same consideration as a drawer frame as regards cross-grain joinery. Just as on the drawer frame, a fixed-in-place shelf, using sliding dovetail joints, will add strength to the project. This is because it ties the sides together structurally.

In most bookcases and other storage cabinets, adjustable shelves should be used. There are many methods for supporting adjustable shelves. The most basic is a series of holes. This method was used for the bookcase (Illus. 10-2). You could either insert pieces of dowel or shelf pins to support the shelf. Shelf pins on the market range from simple, forged-brass library pins to moulded plastic (Illus. 10-3). Some forged-brass pins use brass sleeves inserted into the wood. This method does require very careful placement of the holes. If they don't line up, the shelf will "rock" and not sit solidly.

In some projects, you need adjustable shelves, but need to make sure they stay in

Illus. 10-1.
Note the shelves
and partition on
this bookcase.

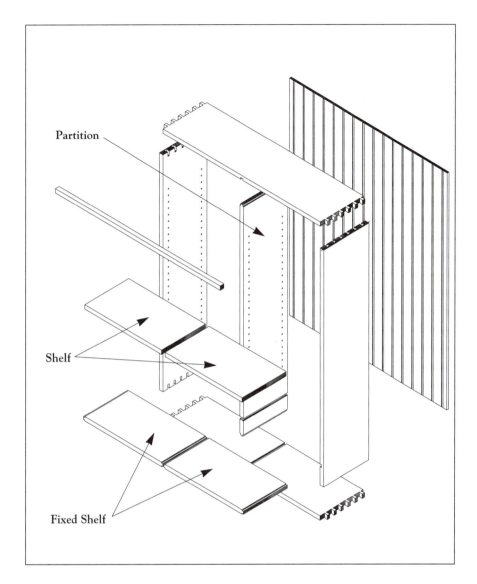

place. Although you can buy moulded-plastic shelf pins that will hold the shelf down, you may want to keep the shelf from sliding out. If the carcass has a face frame, this will not be a problem. If there is no face frame, a groove can be cut along the length of the shelf, on the underside. This groove will sit over any shelf pin (Illus. 10-4).

A common piece of furniture is a curio cabinet. As the name implies, curio cabinets protect various knickknacks and collectibles while displaying them. Many curio cabinets have built-in lights to show off the cabinet's treasures. This often leads to glass shelves to allow the light to pass from one level to another. Although you could spend the money for high-strength glass shelves, you could inset less-expensive glass into a wooden frame (Illus. 10-5). The frame provides support for the glass all around its periphery, not just on a few localized points. The best joint for the frame is a mortise-and-tenon joint.

A common mistake is to make shelves too long. This results in the shelf sagging in its middle, under any weight (Illus. 10-6). This is especially common with plywood or particle-

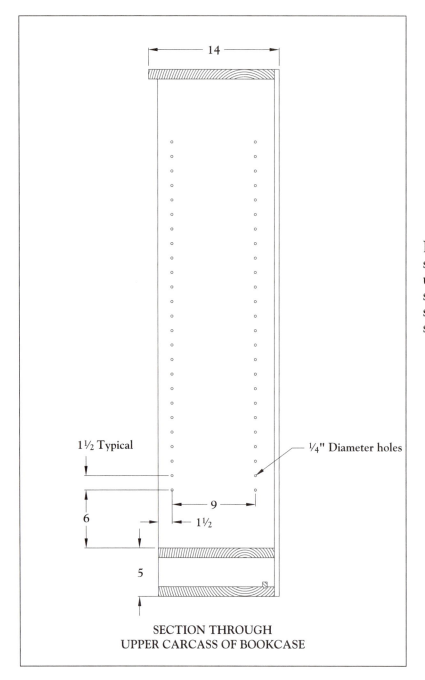

14

1½ Typical

¼" Diameter holes

9

1½

6

5

SECTION THROUGH
UPPER CARCASS OF BOOKCASE

Illus. 10-2. This cross section of the bookcase's upper carcass shows the series of holes used to support adjustable shelves.

board. You're better off limiting your shelves to no more than 3 feet long.

When the shelf has to support heavy items, you could add a stiffening strip or edge banding along the front edge (Illus. 10-7). The technique used to add the stiffener can also be used to add a solid-wood edge strip to a plywood shelf. Although a simple edge-glue joint will work for solid-wood shelves, a tongue-and-groove joint will be necessary for plywood (Illus. 10-8). Another method would be to cut the groove in both the shelf and the reinforce-

Illus. 10-3. A variety of shelf pins.

ment strip and use a spline (Illus. 10-9).

After the stiffener or edge banding is attached to a shelf, it must be trimmed flush. This can be done with a hand plane when the shelf is solid wood. However, if you're using plywood, it would be quite easy to remove the outermost hardwood veneer with a plane. Therefore, the recommended method is to use a table-mounted router with a flush-trimming bit. Mount an auxiliary fence on the standard router table fence. This auxiliary fence is elevated above the tabletop to allow the waste from the reinforcement strip to pass under it as

Illus. 10-4. If you are not using a face frame, you can cut a groove which will fit over any shelf pins.

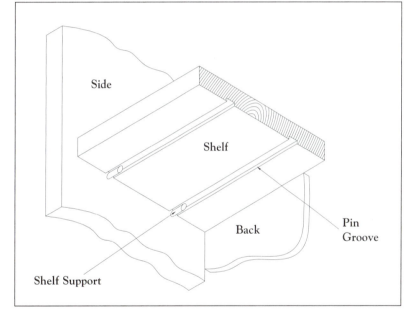

Side

Shelf

Back

Pin Groove

Shelf Support

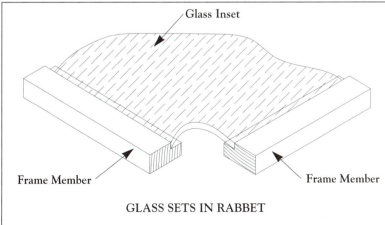

Glass Inset

Frame Member

Frame Member

GLASS SETS IN RABBET

Illus. 10-5. Glass inset into a frame.

the shelf is moved vertically along the fence. Also, the fence is set in the same vertical plane with the flush-trimming router bit.

If you are adding a reinforcing strip, do this before you cut the shelf to final length. This will ensure that the added strip matches at the ends of the shelves.

Many larger cabinets use partitions to break up the spaces. Partitions are nothing more than permanent shelving installed vertically. ◙

Illus. 10-6. If shelves are made too long, they will sag in the middle, as shown here.

Illus. 10-7. A stiffening strip or strengthening spine along the front edge of a shelf will support heavy items.

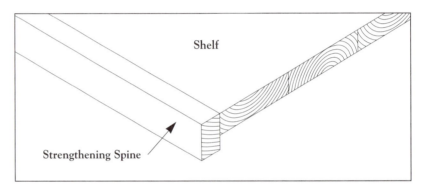

Illus. 10-8. A tongue-and-groove joint is necessary to support heavy items placed on plywood shelves.

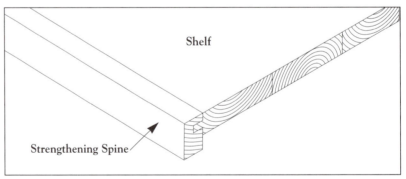

Illus. 10-9. A spline can also be used to support the plywood shelf.

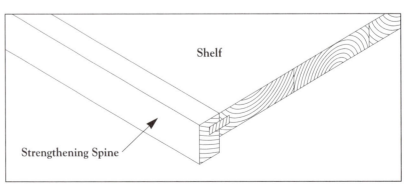

11 DOOR CONSTRUCTION

Doors offer the wood crafter many options. They can be hinged, sliding, sliding tambour (as used in rolltop desks), or "flip" doors.

As discussed in Chapter 1, doors can be built as solid panels of wood, frame-and-panel, glass inset into a frame, or as a tambour (Illus. 11-1). The frame-and-panel door is constructed the same way as the frame-and-panel carcass discussed in Chapter 4.

DOORS WITH SOLID PANELS

When using solid panels of wood as doors, be especially mindful of your material selection. The same considerations apply as were discussed in Chapter 3 for making panels. Use the straightest grain you can find and use relatively narrow boards. Also, alternate the grain for best management of seasonal movement (Illus. 11-2). A plain panel door requires more consideration in these regards, because it doesn't have the benefit of a frame to help control cupping and twist.

An often used method for controlling cupping and twist in panels not otherwise supported is to add a piece across their ends. This is often called a "breadboard end" or "end cap" (Illus. 11-3). By all appearances, placing this strip across the end grain of a panel looks like a flagrant violation of the rules regarding cross-grain joinery. For this reason, there are special techniques used to attach the end cap.

Remember that wood expands and shrinks as it absorbs atmospheric moisture. This moisture is contained in the material which makes up the wood's grain. As a result, the wood will move much more across the width of the board than along its length. The amount of movement is directly relative to the amount of moisture absorbed and the width of the board or panel. Similarly, the amount of stress developed, which would lead to splitting as the wood dries, is relative to the width of board, or panel, not allowed to "float." Simply put, if a board is drying it will shrink across its width. The wider the board, the more it will shrink and the greater the tendency of its edges to move to the middle of the board. By fixing the board in place at several points along the end cap and allowing the wood to "float" between these points, you will divide one large stressed

Illus. 11-1. Various door cross sections.

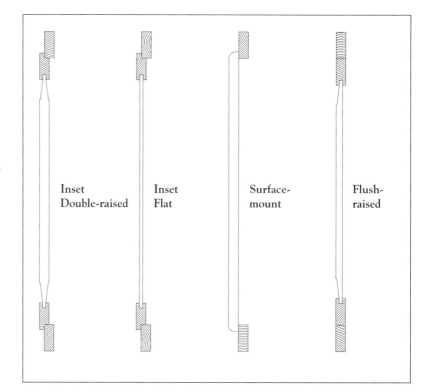

Inset
Double-raised

Inset
Flat

Surface-
mount

Flush-
raised

Illus. 11-2. Use narrow boards with straight grain when making solid-wood doors. Also, alternate the grain pattern of the pieces. This ensures that each piece will move independently.

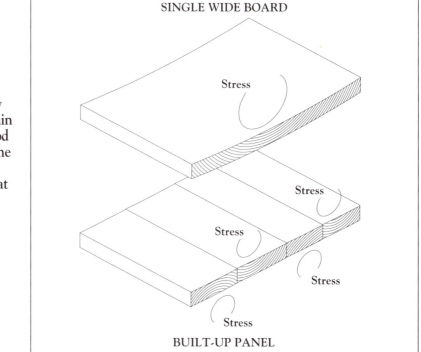

SINGLE WIDE BOARD

Stress

Stress

Stress

Stress

Stress

BUILT-UP PANEL

Illus. 11-3. Panel with breadboard ends.

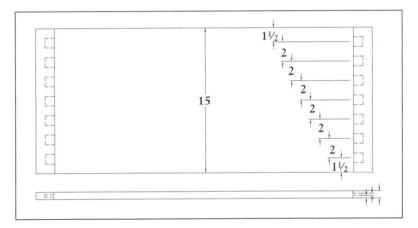

Illus. 11-4. Fixing the board in place at several points along the end cap, and allowing the wood to "float" between these points, breaks one large area of stress down into several smaller ones.

area into several smaller ones. The resulting smaller areas of stress will not be big enough to damage the panel (Illus. 11-4). The worst case would be a glue joint that spans the entire width of the board. In such a case, the wood is not allowed to move at all and either the joint will fail or the panel will split.

Attaching End Caps

The more traditional method of attaching the end cap is to use multiple mortises, as shown in Illus. 11-3. These mortise-and-tenon joints will act to break up the shrinkage/expansion stresses just described. Sometimes, each joint is pegged with dowels in the middle of the tenon, which is cut a little narrow to allow movement even within the mortise.

Making the multiple mortise-and-tenon joint (Illus. 11-5) at first can look difficult. It really isn't. Start by laying out the tongue, which will form the tenons. The next step is to cut the tenons. Try to space them less than 3 inches apart. Some woods, like pine, will move more than others and there should be shorter spans between their joints. Woods considered more "stable" will move less and can have larger spans. To have a shoulder at each end of the joint, you'll have to use an odd number of tenons.

Now, make the mortises. Use the tenon to locate the mortise positions (Illus. 11-6). It would be a good idea to use wood a little thicker than the panel for the mortise board. Cut the mortises using your favorite technique. After the mortised board is permanently attached to the panel, trim it flush with the panel.

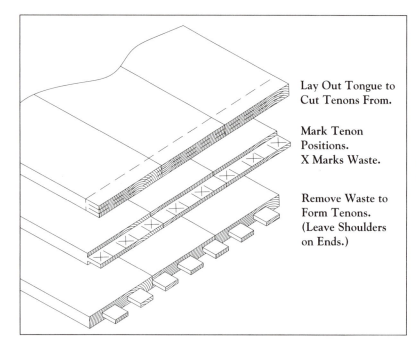

Lay Out Tongue to
Cut Tenons From.

Mark Tenon
Positions.
X Marks Waste.

Remove Waste to
Form Tenons.
(Leave Shoulders
on Ends.)

Illus. 11-5. Sequence for
making the mortise-and-
tenon joint.

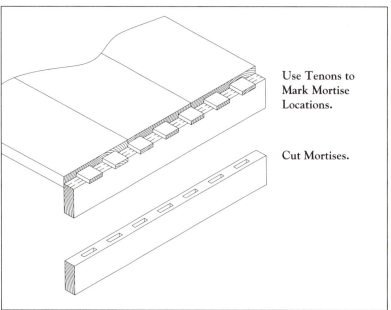

Use Tenons to
Mark Mortise
Locations.

Cut Mortises.

Illus. 11-6. The
sequence for cutting the
mortises.

FRAME-AND-PANEL DOORS

Frame-and-panel doors are very popular (Illus. 11-7). Their construction is no different from that of the frame-and-panel carcass components discussed in Chapter 4. The traditional method used a frame built with mortise-and-tenon joinery. A panel was "raised" by cutting moulding in it with a plane.

Many workshops today have a router and shaper. Both machines offer time savings and ways to create a variety of shapes for panel-raising and stile-and-rail moulding. One of the

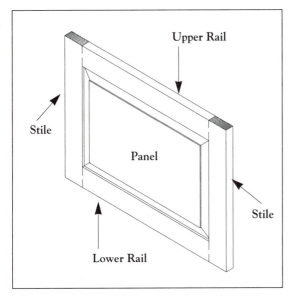

Illus. 11-7. Raised frame-and-panel door.

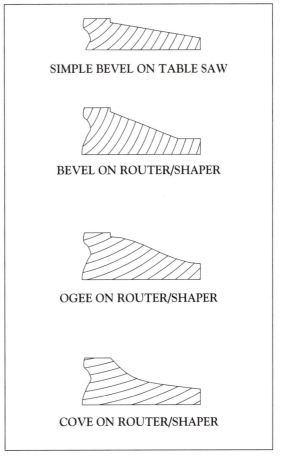

SIMPLE BEVEL ON TABLE SAW

BEVEL ON ROUTER/SHAPER

OGEE ON ROUTER/SHAPER

COVE ON ROUTER/SHAPER

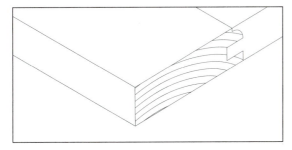

Illus. 11-8. A router-made moulding shape.

Illus. 11-9. The four most commonly used panel-raising shapes.

stile/rail moulding shapes is shown in Illus. 11-8. The four most common panel-raising shapes are shown in Illus. 11-9.

The stile/rail joint isn't very strong. This stems from a lack of long grain to long grain glued area. However, the joint is fine for a typical cabinet door. For anything larger than 18×30 inches, consider some techniques covered in Chapter 4 in which the moulded frame parts are used with a mortise-and-tenon joint. Remember, the frame is the structure supporting the raised panel. Solid panels of oak and other hardwoods get very heavy.

It is common to cut all of the stiles and rails individually to size, and then mould them for assembly. Since the rail bits do leave quite a bit

of tear-out, try to cut boards to length and mould the ends before ripping them to width. After all of the rails are cut to width, use the shaped ends to set the height for the stile bit that moulds the long edges of the parts.

Glass doors also feature frame-and-panel techniques. The difference is the glass is usually set into a rabbet on the back side, rather than a groove. A simple way to do this job is to build a frame with the router using stile/rail bits. After it's assembled, you can use a rabbeting bit to remove the leftover stock on the inside surface. This is made possible by the fact that most of the stile/rail bit sets cut a $\frac{3}{8}$-inch-deep groove which would be matched by the most common $\frac{3}{8}$-inch rabbeting bit. You will have to square up the corners with a chisel.

The traditional glass-panelled door used an unmoulded frame and muntins to hold the glass (Illus. 11-10). The door in our bookcase project uses the more traditional technique.

Many cabinets, like our bookcase, have glass doors divided into separate panels. There are a couple of ways to do this. Illus. 11-11 is a construction drawing for the bookcase door. The frame is not moulded. A muntin is glued around the frame to provide a place to set the glass and add some moulding. The muntin could be shaped with a moulding plane, a scratch stock, a table-saw moulding head, or a router. Some projects call for curved muntins. The only ways to bring the shape around a curve is either with a scratch stock or a scraper. The dividers are little more than thin strips of stock with the muntin glued in place. These strips are set into the door frame members. For best alignment, the matching notches should be cut simultaneously. Clamp the frame members together while cutting them; the cutting should be done before assembling the door frame.

Divided glass-panel doors can also be made with the same router bit sets used for making multi-panel raised panel doors. The dividers are simply narrow intermediate stiles/rails (Illus. 11-12). Just as when you use these router bits on the frame of a door, you'll have to remove that flange of stock on the inside edge to form a rabbet to set the glass in.

The glazing putty may be hard to find, but it is available in some larger hardware stores. You could also use glaziers' clips, which are often found where you would find supplies for framing pictures. I "cheat" and take the finished door to the glass shop. With the door in hand, they can be sure to cut the glass correctly and install it.

INSTALLING THE DOORS

After the doors are made, it's time to install them. Start by making sure the door fits the carcass correctly. The fit can be made especially clean by building the door slightly oversized and trimming it down to final fit with a hand plane .

Hinges take many forms these days. The most common is still the traditional *butt hinge*, as shown in Illus. 11-13. It is available made of formed brass sheet metal or the more-expensive extruded brass. Using undersized hinges is a common mistake. You have to remember those hinges are supporting the weight of the door and have to withstand any abuse that might be inflicted over the years. Less-expensive and undersized hardware will wear quickly. Hinges made of sheet metal are fine as long as you check the thickness of the metal. Pick up one of the woodworker's hardware catalogues that are available and look at the variety you have to choose from.

The butt hinge is used on inset or flush-mounted doors. These doors can be used with or without a face frame. If a face frame is used, the knuckle or pivot part of the hinge goes on the front of the cabinet. If no face frame is used, as on the upper carcass of our bookcase, the hinge knuckles may be placed on the sides of the carcass.

There are a couple of ways to install butt

Illus. 11-10. Bookcase door with unmoulded frames and muntins.

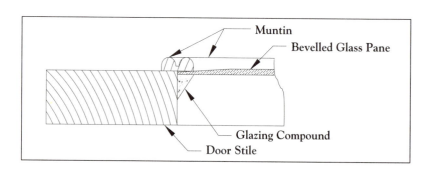

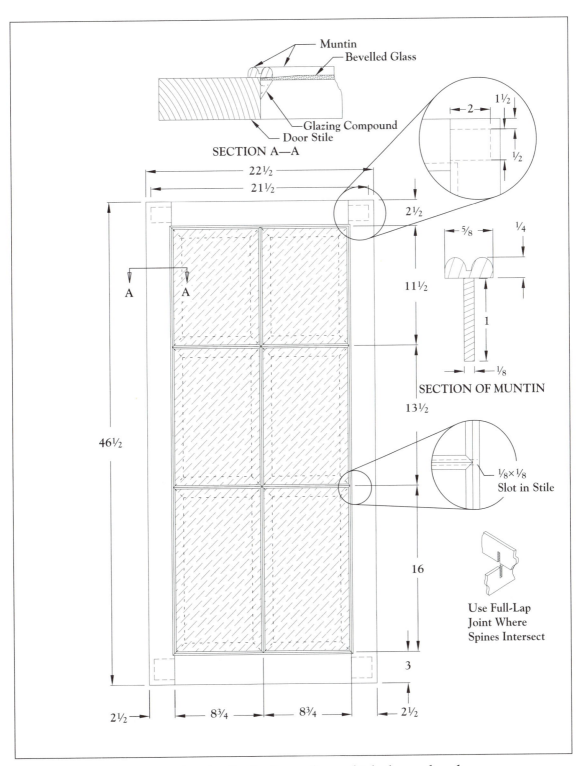

Muntin
Bevelled Glass
Glazing Compound
Door Stile
SECTION A—A

SECTION OF MUNTIN

Use Full-Lap
Joint Where
Spines Intersect

$\frac{1}{8} \times \frac{1}{8}$
Slot in Stile

Illus. 11-11. Construction drawing for bookcase door, which shows glass doors divided into separate panels.

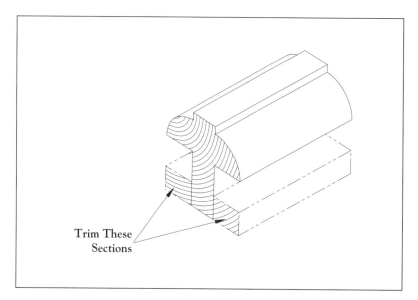

Illus. 11-12. Dividers for glass-panel doors.

Trim These Sections

Illus. 11-13. The butt hinge is the most common hinge used on cabinet doors.

Illus. 11-14. A hinge set in place.

hinges. Either way, butt hinges need to be mortised into the hinge stile of the door and the carcass or face frame. This is one of those situations when preparing to do the job with a machine takes longer than doing the job by hand. However, the extra time may be well-invested for someone lacking the steadiness of hand that comes with experience. Using a router also is helpful when installing several hinges.

We'll start with the hand method. Locate the hinge placement. For simplicity, align the top edge of the top hinge with the bottom of the upper rail, and the bottom edge of the lower hinge with the top of the lower rail. For larger doors, you may want to add a third hinge centered between these two. Draw a reference line on the edge of the door as just described. Make sure the line is continued to both the door and carcass. Use the actual hinge to mark the other end of the mortise. Lay the hinge in the door as shown in Illus. 11-14. Trace the outline of the hinge leaf as it lies on the door stile or carcass. Set a marking gauge to just less than the diameter of the hinge knuckle. Be careful to not go too deep. It's always easier to trim a little more later than to add material.

When the parts are marked out, cut the mortise by making several cross-grain cuts

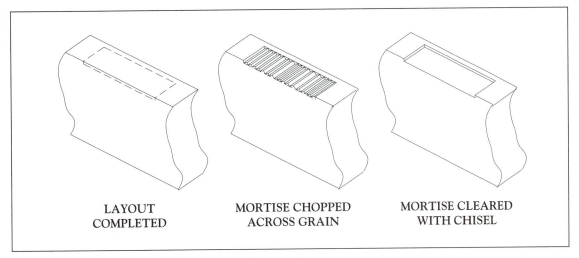

LAYOUT
COMPLETED

MORTISE CHOPPED
ACROSS GRAIN

MORTISE CLEARED
WITH CHISEL

Illus. 11-15. Sequence for cutting and clearing the mortise.

with the chisel (Illus. 11-15). Then, clean the mortise out with a shaving action with the chisel. Do this *slowly*. It's easier to trim a little more as needed than do it again from scratch or put in some fillers to fill the mortise around the hinge. Do not go all the way to the edges of the mortise until the final clearing cut. At that point, you can dress up the edges and make sure that the mortise fits with the hinge leaf.

After the mortises are prepared for the hinges in the door stile, repeat the process on the carcass using the same locator line you started with on the door.

A simple jig could also be made for use with a router. The main drawback of these jigs is in their limitation to a single hinge size. The jig requires the use of a guide bushing installed in the router base plate. A straight router bit is used. Mark the depth of the mortise using a marking gauge exactly as done when cutting the joint by hand. Adjust the router bit to match the layout line when mounting the jig on the stock.

Illus. 11-16 shows the router jig. It's little more than a flat plate made of hardboard, plywood, or acrylic with a rectangular section removed. The length of this section is calculated by adding the difference between the outside diameter of the guide bushing and the router bit to the actual hinge-leaf dimension. The width is calculated by adding half the guide-bushing offset and the hinge size. The plate is attached to a piece of hardwood clamped in place for use. When using this type of device for making the mortises, it will be necessary to establish centerlines for the mortises rather than lay out the actual hinge size. Also, a centerline will be marked on the jig, and all you have to do is align the centerlines.

When using this type of jig, tear-out is a common problem along the open edge of the mortise. This tear-out can be drastically reduced by making the first pass from right to left and making a cut about 1/8 inch wide. Then use the template to guide the bushing to clean out the mortise. The router bit will leave rounded corners that must be squared up with a chisel.

There are hinges made especially for the rabbetted or inset doors (Illus. 11-17). Until just a couple of years ago, these were the most common types of door used in factory-made kitchen and bath cabinetry. They have since been replaced by the surface-mount door. Surface-mount doors use hinges identical to the inset type, but without the offset formed on the door leaf. Neither of these types of hinge requires mortises. A popular version of these hinges incorporates a spring which makes the doors "self closing."

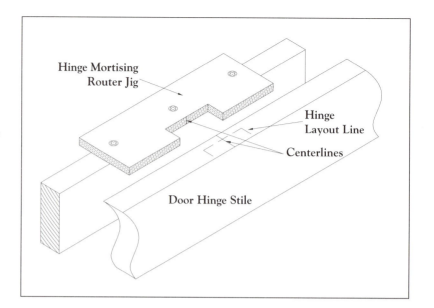

Illus. 11-16. This router jig can be used to cut mortises for hinges.

Illus. 11-17. Offset hinges.

Hinges that are not visible are becoming more popular. The user should refer to the instructions provided with the hardware.

Not all doors are mounted on hinges. Flip-and-slide doors pivot and slide out of the way. These doors are most widely recognized as used in the traditional barrister's bookcase shown in Illus. 1–11. They actually require no hardware except some dowel pegs, although there are some hardware devices on the market that provide hinge points and ball-bearing tracks.

Ball bearing tracks aside, the flip-and-slide

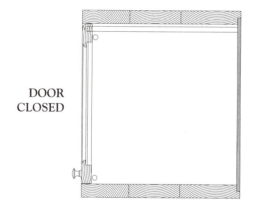

DOOR
CLOSED

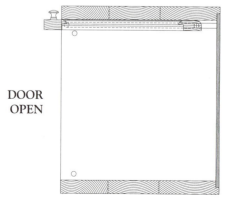

DOOR
OPEN

Illus. 11-18. The mechanism for the flip-and-slide door.

door is easy to install using the traditional methods. All they require are six dowel pins and dadoes that have to be cut in the carcass sides. Illus. 11-18 shows how the dowel pins in the door travel in the dado on the carcass side. The dowel pins in the carcass side support the door when open, and keep it in position when closed. Notice how the top of the door is radiused so its swing will not be impeded.

Flip-and-slide doors can also be installed so the door is attached along the side of the cabinet and slides back into the cabinet. These type of door are popular for video cabinets because they can be closed to conceal the television set and pushed out of the way when the television set is being watched. ◨

12 DRAWERS

Drawers also come in a variety of design styles and construction techniques (Illus. 12-1). The choices include whether the front of the drawer will overhang or be flush with the carcass or drawer support frames, as shown in Illus. 12-2. This is usually the first decision to be made, and it will affect all other aspects of the drawer design, which includes selecting a way to keep the drawer from going in too far when it is closed. When the drawer front overhangs the front of the carcass, it will act as a stop. If flush-fitting drawers are being used, a drawer stop has to be glued in place on the drawer frame.

The next decision involves how the drawers are actually built, specifically, what type of joint will be used between the sides and front of the drawer. Dovetail, box, offset tongue-and-groove, or rabbet joints can be used. Making each of these joints is discussed in Chapter 3, so we won't do it here. Instead, we'll discuss the merits of each and where they might be used.

The main consideration is that the joint connecting the front of drawers to the sides must bear the weight of a moving drawer and its contents. With that in mind, the bigger the drawer, or heavier the contents, the stronger the joint needs to be.

The *rabbet joint* (Illus. 12-3) should only be used on small drawers. Applications might include small jewelry chests or other chests where the height of the drawer does not exceed a couple of inches. As discussed in chapter 3, end grain is glued to long grain when a rabbet joint is used. This makes a poor glue joint.

Dovetail joints are the traditional joints used to attach the front of drawers to the sides. A half-blind dovetail joint (Illus. 12-4) is the strongest joint to use in this application because of the mechanical interlock it provides. The joint is hidden when the drawer is closed. Drawers which use a lip around their fronts will have the dovetail joint set into a rabbet. There are several manufacturers of

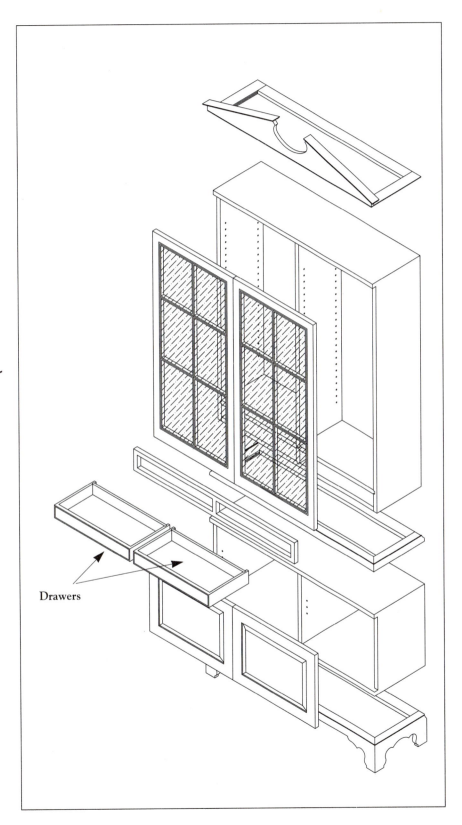

Illus. 12-1. An exploded view of the bookcase showing its drawers.

Drawers

Illus. 12-2.
Some drawer designs.

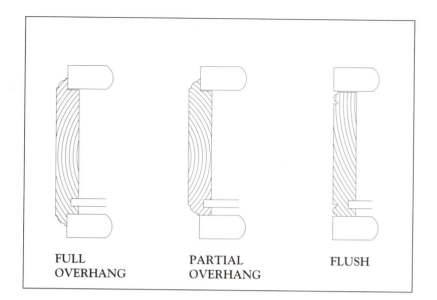

FULL
OVERHANG

PARTIAL
OVERHANG

FLUSH

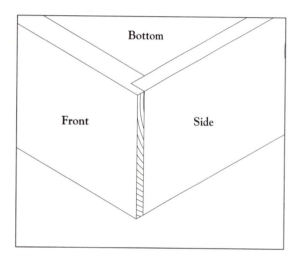

Illus. 12-3. The rabbet joint as used
on a drawer.

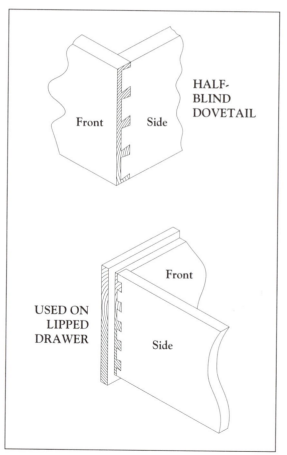

HALF-
BLIND
DOVETAIL

USED ON
LIPPED
DRAWER

Illus. 12-4. A half-blind dovetail joint.

dovetail jigs for use with routers on the market. The half-blind dovetail shown in Illus. 12-4 is made by hand in the same manner as the half-blind dovetails used for carcass construction, which are discussed in Chapter 3.

Box, or finger, joints are used in utilitarian applications. Because of their glue surface and the reliability of modern glues, the box joint is quite strong. A problem with this joint is revealed when the drawer bottom is installed.

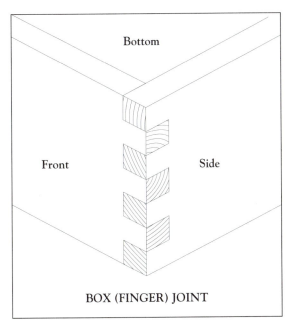

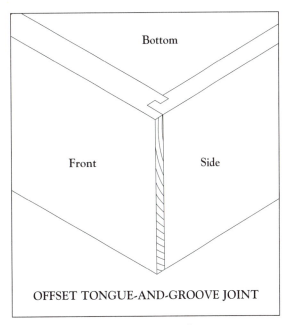

Illus. 12-5. A box joint.

Illus. 12-6. Offset tongue-and-groove joint.

As shown in Illus. 12-5, it's difficult to hide the slot formed inside the box to house the drawer bottom. It would be visible as a square hole on one of the boards. As a result, the common practice is to glue a plywood bottom directly to the front, sides, and back to form the box joint. For this reason, the use of the box joint should be limited to small-to-medium-size drawers, to avoid problems that occur when solid wood moves (through the seasons) relative to the plywood. Also, when box joints are used, they are typically used on the front and back of the drawer.

The *offset tongue-and-groove joint* is another joint used for small-to-medium-size drawers. As you can see in Illus. 12-6, there is some mechanical lock between the side and front of the drawer, but unlike that on the dovetail joint, this interlock does not rely on the best orientation of grain. The result is the possibility that the tongue on the side boards will split off.

FALSE FRONTS

Projects such as filing cabinets or specialty storage cabinets sometimes require large drawer fronts. At other times, we'll want a drawer to look like a door. These are situations where false fronts should be used. False fronts are usually of frame-and-panel construction, to fit the panel sizes needed and control seasonal movement.

The basic technique involved in using a false front is to build a box using secondary wood and attach the front by using either the bolts used to attach the drawer-pull hardware or screws from inside the box. You'll have to remember that the panels in frame-and-panel construction are seldom even with the frame. The gap formed by this unevenness will have to be filled before the front can be attached to the drawer. Some options are as follow: cut a wooden spacer to act as a bridge; cut a rabbet around the front of the drawer, to inset the drawer within the frame; or make attachments through frame members. These are only a few possible solutions to the problem.

False fronts also lend themselves to mass production. The front does not have to be of frame-and-panel construction. Solid-wood panels of different species can be attached to the boxes, to meet demand.

CONSTRUCTION TECHNIQUES

Drawer bottoms are set into grooves let into the sides and front of the drawer (Illus. 12-7). One-quarter -inch-thick plywood is the most common material used for drawer bottoms these days. The traditional material was a ¼- to ½-inch-thick solid-wood panel. The thicker panels were tapered around the front and side edges, to fit into the groove. This tapering was done with a hand plane. Today, you could set up a jig for the table saw such as that used to make a straight, bevelled, raised panel.

As mentioned earlier, you could use the same joint to attach the backs of drawers as you do the front, but this joint will not have to withstand the same amount of stress as the front, nor will it have to be aesthetically pleas-ing. The most common technique is a dado groove let into the sides, as shown in Illus. 12-7. Notice how the back rests on the drawer bottom. The back is usually attached by nailing it through its sides. Don't rely on a glue joint to do the job. (Again, end grain mates with long grain on this joint, and the end grain makes a poor surface for a glue bond.)

Install the bottom in the slots cut in the drawer sides and front. Don't use any glue on the bottom. Use the bottom to position the back in the dadoes, and nail it in place using small nails driven through the drawer sides. After the back is nailed in place, you'll notice that there is still some flexibility in the assembly. Make sure that the drawer is square by checking the measurements diagonally across the drawer. Make any necessary adjustments by maneuvering the parts. When the drawer is square, drive several nails through the bottom

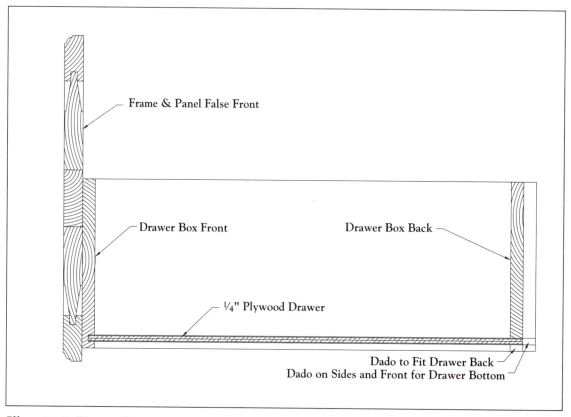

Illus. 12-7. Drawer bottoms are set into grooves cut into the sides and front of the drawer.

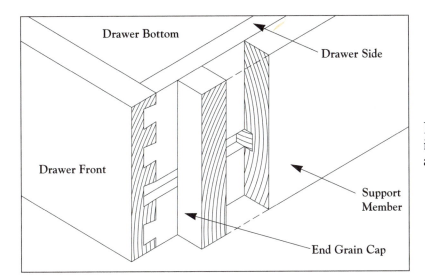

Drawer Bottom

Drawer Side

Drawer Front

Support Member

End Grain Cap

Illus. 12-8. This drawer is supported by a dado and runner.

and into the back. This will provide what engineers call a "shear panel" and stiffen the drawer.

Some people will want to use the box (or finger) or through dovetail joints, for aesthetic purposes. When doing this, you'll want to hide the slot used to house the drawer bottom. With the through dovetail and box joints, there are a couple of ways to do that. First, since the major consideration is what's visible when the drawer is closed, plan your joint so that the hole is on the side of the drawer.

Second, you could use a router to form a rabbet, and glue the drawer bottom in the rabbet. You'll need to use a router table to support the drawer and router. Since you are gluing all around the periphery of the drawer, this technique should be limited to small-to-medium drawers because of the potential problems of the drawer moving relative to the bottom over the seasons.

The router will leave a radius in the corner that needs to be squared up with a chisel. Avoid the temptation to use a mallet to drive the chisel. This is not the time to split the wood. Use a paring motion with your hands only. Cut the drawer bottom *after* you have made the rabbet. This way, you can cut the bottom to fit the opening precisely.

In Chapter 5, we learned how to build and

install internal frames. These frames are the most common way to support drawers, and they are the traditional method. As the wood dries and is worn, it is common for the drawer to start to stick and not work smoothly. The answer is to rub the bottom and side of the drawers and the tops of the drawer frames with candle wax or paraffin. There are several pieces of plastic hardware on the market to make the drawers slide over the frame smoothly and guide them in and out with guide rails. These are usually made of nylon, and are common in the less-expensive furniture and cabinets you might find in department stores.

It is a common practice to install dust panels. Such panels are usually made of $1/4$-inch-thick plywood. They are let into a groove cut on the internal periphery of the frame. Dust panels are most common in the bottom frame when a carcass has no bottom. This is often the case in chests of drawers for clothing.

Drawers can also be supported by cutting a dado along the length of the side of the drawer (Illus. 12-8). This dado is then slid over a runner set into the side of a carcass. Such an arrangement is often used for small chests of drawers where drawer support frames are not needed as structural braces in the carcass.

When supporting drawers in a carcass, it's important to stop the support runner in back

Illus. 12-9. Drawer slide.

of the front edge of the carcass side. One method would be to cut the dado across the full width of the carcass side and glue a strip on the front. The strip should be at least as thick as the distance the dado in the drawer side is set back from the front of the drawer. You could also use any of the methods for stopped dadoes mentioned earlier.

Illus. 12-8 shows how this system works. A section of the drawer support rail suspends the drawer from beneath a tabletop. In such a case, a piece of wood is glued over the end (front) of the support board to hide the end grain. This is often taken from the same board as the drawer front to give the appearance of a single board.

Just as the drawer in a basic drawer frame, this drawer can be made to operate more smoothly by rubbing some candle wax or paraffin into the runner. Since the dado is only cut in the drawer side, the front will act as a stop to keep the drawer from going too far when closed.

Drawer Slides

Today, the trend is to use more drawer slides (Illus. 12-9). These are mechanical hardware devices intended to support the drawer and make it function smoothly. The advantage is that they generally work pretty well, depending on the quality of drawer slides one buys. The disadvantages are that they are fairly expensive as they increase in quality and that they are quite visible. The sight of a ball-bearing, pol-ished silver drawer slide on the side of a drawer in a Federal or Shaker style chest of drawers ruins the entire effect for many "purists."

Essentially, the heavier the drawer, the more consideration one should give to using a drawer slide. This is also true of furniture for commercial offices which is not likely to receive the occasional application of wax to the frames and drawers. Also, commercial office furniture can expect harsher treatment than home furniture.

I won't try to explain the installation of the drawer slide, because each manufacturer has its own instructions. The slides are usually rated as to *full or partial extension*, which refers to how far the slide will allow the drawer to open, and their *load* capacity, which refers to how much weight the slide pair will handle. Be sure to include the weight of the drawer with the contents when figuring out the load rating you need. A full-extension slide will allow the drawer to be opened completely, so the back of the drawer comes forward to the front of the opening on the carcass. If the slide has an extension that's less than "full," the back of the drawer stays within the carcass. How much of the back stays within the carcass depends on the extension rating. As a rule, full extension requires a stronger drawer slide because of the way the load stresses are distributed. To decide load rating, estimate how much the drawer and its contents will weigh, and double that number, for safety. ◘

13 STACKING CARCASSES

After the carcasses, base frame, and drawers are built, it's time to assemble them (Illus. 13-1). Carcasses need to be stacked, and on larger projects like our bookcase should not be permanently connected. This allows then to be moved more easily.

Carcasses can be stacked in several ways. One way is to add a joining frame. The frame will provide an aesthetic as well as structural transition between the two carcasses. When the mating surface is a frame, the joining frame can be bolted or screwed directly to it.

The bookcase uses a panel on the bottom of the upper carcass and a panel on top of the lower carcass. When the mating surface is a panel, seasonal movement between the frame and the carcass must be considered. The most common method is to use slotted holes for the attachment screws.

When cutting the joining frame, wait until the carcasses are complete and use them to mark the frame parts for size. This will eliminate errors in transferring measurements. Allow the rails to overhang the lower carcasses slightly. It's a lot easier to trim the rail to fit than to trim the carcass. Mount the upper carcass on the lower one and center it. Mark the rail to the distance between the edges of the upper and lower carcasses. This will establish the distance from the rabbet cheek to the edge of the rail. Now, cut the rabbet for the upper carcass.

When both joining surfaces are panels, dowels can be used to align them. Dowels are often used in china cabinets or when putting mirror frames on dressing tabletops. This will not provide a permanent attachment, but it will keep the two pieces properly aligned.

To use the dowels, drill one side of the joint. Place a dowel center in these holes and mount the mating cabinet in position. The dowel centers will mark the mating part to locate holes for the other side of the joint.

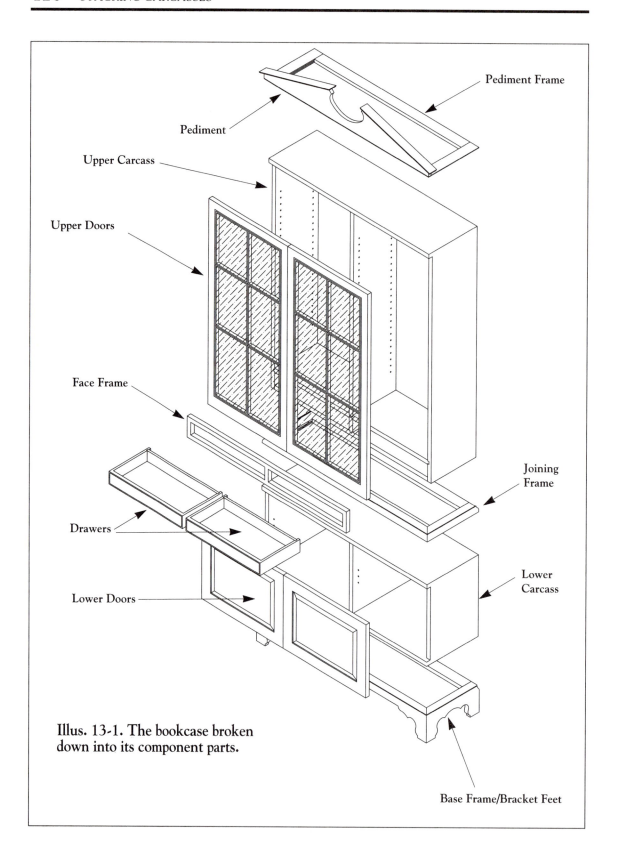

Pediment Frame

Pediment

Upper Carcass

Upper Doors

Face Frame

Joining Frame

Drawers

Lower Carcass

Lower Doors

Illus. 13-1. The bookcase broken down into its component parts.

Base Frame/Bracket Feet

Make certain the drill is perpendicular to the panels when boring the holes. If not, misalignment will make it next to impossible to seat the dowels in both carcasses. Similarly, limiting the number of dowels will decrease the risk of misalignment. Two dowels should be more than adequate.

Another, and perhaps the simplest, method for stacking furniture parts is to use hardware that fastens to the back of both pieces. These are usually simple metal straps. These parts are commonly used in furniture factories to mount mirrors on top of dressers. Like dowels, this hardware does have the advantage of allowing quick assembly or disassembly for moving. ◨

14 DEVELOPING PROJECT PLANS

The most important tool you can use in building a piece of furniture will not cut any wood or perform any other wood-working activity. That tool is your mind. Before you start cutting or shaping any wood, build the project in your mind's eye with a complete set of drawings, a list of all parts, a complete bill of materials, and a well thought-out written plan for executing the project. By spending the time to develop a project plan, you can avoid some common disasters in the shop. Every major corporation that produces anything from toasters to interplanetary space-craft develops plans before building the project. These plans are used as a checklist to ensure that the product is built per the engineer's design. You'll also find such plans in various levels of detail in woodworking books and magazines.

Working without a set of drawings or a cutting list can drive the cost of a project up when you have to buy more lumber to redo some of the work. Also, if you spend a little time developing the written plan, and follow it, you'll save time in the shop. Many readers may consider developing a written plan too time-consuming. Which would take more time and expense: making drawings and writ-

ing these lists or buying more lumber and redoing several steps of construction? A well thought-out plan will help you do the project right the first time.

With the growing popularity of the personal computer these days, many people are starting to use them for creating the "project file." There are many computer-aided design (CAD) software packages on the market that would make making drawings less of a chore. A word processor would take care of the other parts of the file.

The first element of a project file is a complete set of drawings. If done by hand, the drawings should be drawn at full scale. This can take a lot of paper, but it will avoid possible errors in scaling the dimensions. Be sure to include such details as joinery and to show any "hidden lines" for tenons in mortises, etc. If you forget those tenons are there, you're going to cut many parts too short. Always double-check your dimensions. Any error at this point will continue throughout the project.

There are two approaches to designing a piece of furniture. Sometimes, you may want a bookcase to fit in a particular space in your house. Here, start your drawing on the outside of the furniture piece and work your way in.

Although this will give you a piece that will fit where you want to put it, the drawers and shelf sizes will be established after the piece is designed. At other times, you may want a display or storage cabinet with a particular size of cupboard or drawer space. Here you'll want to start the drawings at the space you want defined and work your way out. Obviously, with this type of project, the outside dimensions will be established after the piece is designed.

Whichever is the case for you, start your drawings from the critical dimensions and fill in the pieces and parts to make the furniture project "work." At this point in the book, you'll be able to specify what parts you'll need.

Make certain that the drawings include such critical details as door stops to keep flush doors from travelling into the carcass when you close them. Also, when you use flush drawers, you'll need something to stop the drawers flush with the carcass when they are closed. These stops are often overlooked and can cause a headache if you have to add them later.

Table 14-1. Cutting list.

CUTTING LIST

Item Number	Part Name	Quantity	Material	Thickness (inches)	Width (inches)	Length (inches)	Note

After you've completed your drawings, you need to make a cutting list. A cutting list is essentially a listing of *all* of the wooden parts you need to build your project. The list should include the following information for each piece:
1. Identification of part.
2. Quantity needed.
3. Material specification. (Is the part to be made from primary or secondary wood? Will it be solid lumber or plywood?)
4. Thickness of part.
5. Width of part.
6. Length of part. (Do you need to add anything for joinery?)
7. Any special notes you want to remember for that piece. (Are these rough sizes that will be trimmed to match another part later?)

Get your data directly from your drawings and double-check it. Make sure *all* of the parts are included in the list. Don't forget such things as drawer stops, drawer guides, and glue blocks.

Table 14-2. Bill of materials.

BILL OF MATERIALS

Item Number	Description	Quantity	Vendor	Unit Cost	Total Cost

After you have a cutting list and drawings, you can start to develop a bill of materials. The bill of materials will be your shopping list for buying everything you'll need to build the project. This is where you list *everything* from lumber to glue to hinges and drawer pulls to finishing supplies. Be sure to keep information about where you plan to get the supplies.

Go to your cutting list and add up the area of the stock in square inches. Be sure to separate the stock into primary and secondary woods and then into various thicknesses you'll need. After you've calculated the total area in square inches, divide that number by 144 to arrive at square footage. Most hardwood is available in random width and random length. You can also buy it in dimensioned stock like 1×6's, but you will pay a premium. I recently priced some red oak and found out the dimensioned lumber cost four times the random width and length.

Now is the time to make scrappage allowances. Scrap wood is the wood left over after you cut the lumber to the dimensions needed. You are going to need a scrap allowance whether you buy random width/length or dimensional lumber. To allow for scrap wood, you need to buy a little extra. I've heard suggestions ranging from 20 to 50 percent more.

As a rule, you might want to consider a larger percentage for smaller projects. In fact, for a small box or chest you may want to buy double the amount needed. This is because you can't be certain how the boards will cut and glue up into panels, and the smaller the amount of stock you buy, the less leeway you'll have. Save your scrap and after a few projects you may have enough for another project. Or, you could use those materials in your next project.

CONSTRUCTION PLAN

After the drawings, cutting list, and bill of materials are completed, it's time to write the construction plan. Let's use our bookcase project to write a sample plan. The plan needs to be thorough. Write it as though you are telling someone else how to build it, and that person is someone you don't want to anger because the project does not come together correctly. Do not omit anything.

If you buy a published plan, study the construction instructions. You will almost invariably choose other techniques to fit your particular shop and preferences. To adapt to these differences, you'll have to modify the plan accordingly. Writing your own plan will also give you a chance to develop a better understanding of the project.

When creating a construction plan, write down the major parts that have to be built: upper carcass, upper carcass doors, joining frame, lower carcass, lower carcass doors, drawers, base frame/bracket feet, and pediment. Illus. 14-1 shows the bookcase broken into its component parts.

The bookcase has eight major sections and all of them need to be covered. Take them one at a time. For example, the upper carcass will need the following: top, sides, bottom, partition, back, facing strip, and fascia. Illus. 14-2 shows the upper carcass broken into its component parts.

The top, sides, bottom, shelves, and partition have to be glued-up panels. Always start gluing up panels by selecting the stock for color and grain uniformity. A board in the panel that stands out will always remind you why matching color and grain is important. After the stock is selected, it has to be jointed and glued up to form the panel. Often, you'll be able to get both sides or the top and bottom in one panel. They can be cut into final sizes later. What steps would you go through to make the panels? Write them down.

With the panels finished, the next step will be to get joints ready and cut any grooves, dadoes, or holes called for in the drawings. You could get very detailed on the steps for cutting the joints, depending on the method you choose to employ. If you're cutting dovetails by hand, for example, you could list just about every cut in sequence. Or, you could simply say that the joint needs to be prepared. It's a lot easier to work on the individual parts

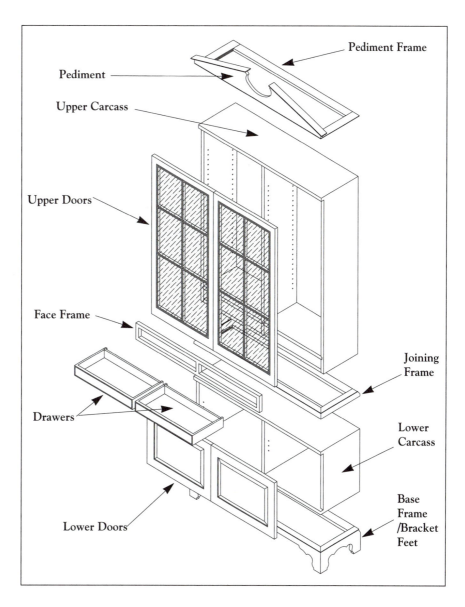

Illus. 14-1. The bookcase and its component parts.

for grooves, rabbets, etc., before they're assembled. When the parts are completed, describe the steps you'll use to assemble them. Will you need to check the carcass for square before gluing it up? If so, explain how.

The upper carcass in our bookcase also needs a fascia or facing frame. There are no panels to glue up here. Just cut some parts per the drawing and cutting list and assemble them. Write down the steps you plan to use. Think about building the fascia slightly over-

sized so it can be trimmed for a perfect fit after it's mounted on the carcass. The same tactic can be used for the facing strip on the top front of the carcass.

The back of the carcass is composed of several boards ripped to width, moulded, and cut to length. Write how you plan to do these.

Continue this process of breaking the project down into major components until you get to the most basic parts. If you have a personal computer with a word processor at your

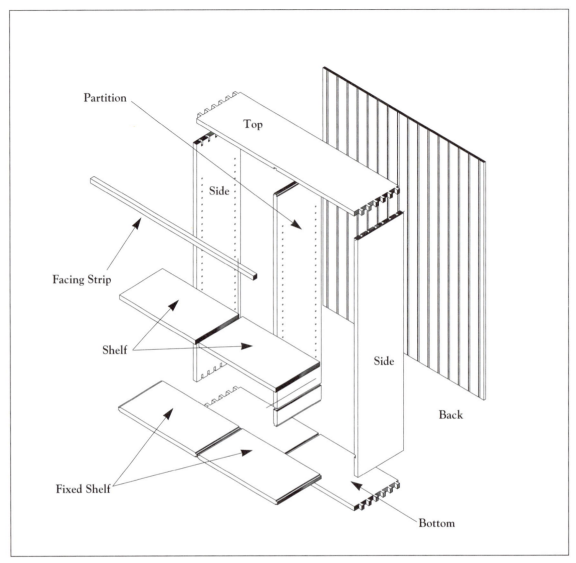

Illus. 14-2. The upper carcass broken down into its component parts.

disposal, you'll find it a big help to use an outline format. As you're writing your plan, you might want to make notes on the side about what tools you plan or need to use.

After all of the major components have been built, there is still one critical step. Finishing demands the same detail in your plan as constructing the carcasses or doors. I've seen some work where stain was applied over installed hinges. It doesn't look very good. Remember that you want to apply an equal amount of finish on all surfaces.

After you've completed and studied the project file, go ahead and order your supplies for the bill of materials and start cutting wood. Follow your project plan, checking off each instruction as you go. With a well thought-out project plan, you can start with sorting lumber and follow the instructions right up until you are moving the project in from the shop. ◘

15 BUILDING THE BOOKCASE

This chapter contains the project file for the bookcase we've been using as a study aid (Illus. 15-1). This bookcase is based on a Chippendale design, and should look good just about anywhere. It is a good project on which to test the techniques you learned in the previous chapters. Because of the size of the project and the amount of lumber involved, I strongly suggest that you practice your techniques on some pine before tackling it. You may want to wait until you've built a few smaller projects before trying this one. I have selected joinery for this project file. If you feel you would like to use other methods, go ahead, but be sure to adjust the project file to adapt to your changes.

When examining the cutting list on page 142, you will see there are 94 parts that need to be cut and joined to make the project. This does not include the individual boards which are jointed and glued up to make the various panels. Remember, the key to overcoming the intimidation of a complex project is to build one part at a time. The project file defines the parts with drawings and a cutting list. Follow the instructions in the construction plan one

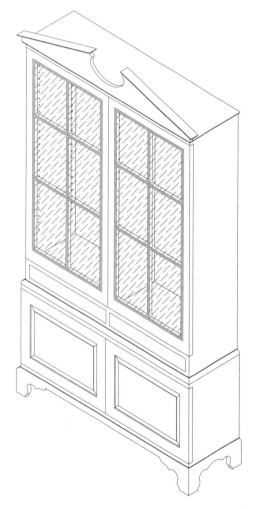

Illus. 15-1. This chapter contains project-file information for building this bookcase.

step at a time. As each step is finished, check it off and move on to the next step.

It would be a good idea to take the doors to a glass shop to be glazed. The bill of materials, which appears on page 145, calls for bevelled glass windows. The glazier will want to cut each piece to fit the doors.

CONSTRUCTION PLAN

Building the Upper Carcass (Illus. 15-2)

1. Select panel stock that is uniform in color and grain.
2. Joint and glue up panels for the sides. Make sure that all the panels end up about ¼ inch wider than needed and an inch or so longer, to allow for final trimming to size later.
3. Joint and glue up panels for the top.
4. Joint and glue up panels for the shelves and partition.
5. Joint and glue up a panel of secondary wood for the bottom.
6. Joint and glue up panels for the fixed shelf.
7. Use a scraper to remove excess glue that squeezed out when panels were clamped up. Do *not* try to sand it off because the glue will wreck a sanding belt.
8. Sand or plane the panels flat and level.
9. Trim the panels to size as indicated in the cutting list on page 142.
10. Mark the panels with chalk to identify which face you will want to use on the outside of the carcass. Put the best face out on sides, down on the top, and up on the fixed shelves.
11. Cut rabbets on back of the sides for backing boards, as indicated in Illus. 15-2.
12. Bore ¼-inch holes for support pins for the adjustable shelves as indicated in Illus. 15-2.
13. Cut half-blind dovetails to join the top and bottom to the sides.
14. Cut sliding dovetails in the top and bottom panels to install the partition.
15. Cut sliding dovetails in the sides and partition to install fixed shelves.
16. Cut and shape the drawer stop rail as indicated in Illus. 15-2.
17. Prepare a dado on the inside face of the bottom panel for the drawer stops.
18. Glue the drawer stops in place.
19. Scrape or sand (to 180 grit) the inside faces of the carcass parts before assembly. Be careful to keep the panels level and flat.
20. Assemble the top and bottom to the sides.
21. Check the bookcase for square by taking diagonal measurements.
22. If necessary, cut a piece of plywood or Masonite to set into the rabbets cut into the side carcass. This plywood or Masonite will hold the bookcase square while the glue cures.
23. Glue the partition in place. Apply glue only to the front 2 to 3 inches of dovetail joint and wipe off the excess glue with a damp sponge.
24. Install the fixed shelves using the same method as for the partition.
25. Cut the facing strip.
26. Glue and clamp the facing strip into place.
27. Plane or sand the facing strip flush with the top panel.

Building the Fascia (Illus. 15-3)

1. Cut material for the stiles and rails as indicated in the cutting list.
2. Form tenons on the rails and the intermediate stile.
3. Cut mortises in the stiles and rails.
4. Glue and clamp the mortise-and-tenon joints.

Installing the Fascia on the Carcass

1. Align the upper rail with the top of the fixed shelves and center the stile with the partition.

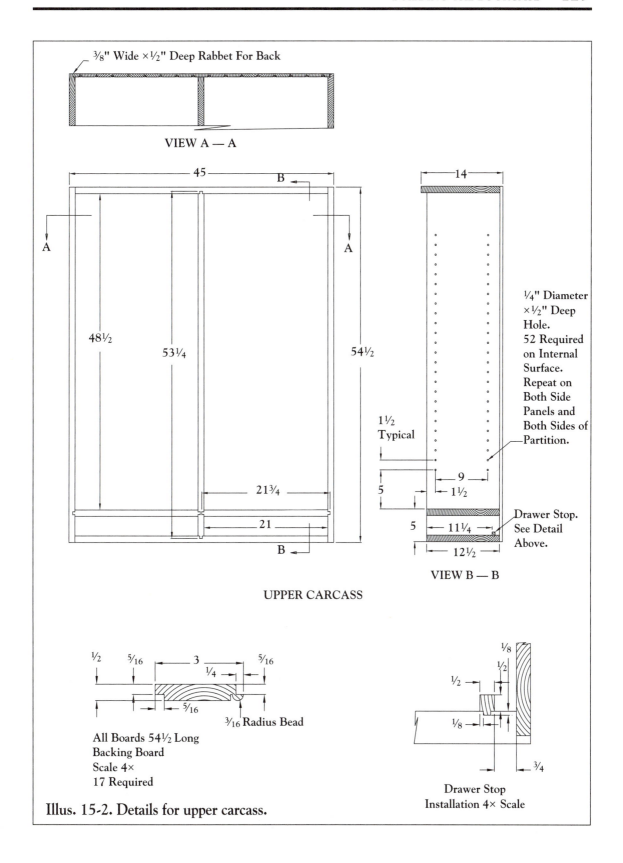

³⁄₈" Wide ×¹⁄₂" Deep Rabbet For Back

VIEW A — A

45

B

A   A

48¹⁄₂

53¹⁄₄

54¹⁄₂

21³⁄₄

21

B

UPPER CARCASS

14

¹⁄₄" Diameter ×¹⁄₂" Deep Hole. 52 Required on Internal Surface. Repeat on Both Side Panels and Both Sides of Partition.

1¹⁄₂ Typical

5

9

1¹⁄₂

5   11¹⁄₄

12¹⁄₂

Drawer Stop. See Detail Above.

VIEW B — B

¹⁄₂   ⁵⁄₁₆   3   ⁵⁄₁₆

¹⁄₄

⁵⁄₁₆

³⁄₁₆ Radius Bead

All Boards 54¹⁄₂ Long
Backing Board
Scale 4×
17 Required

¹⁄₈

¹⁄₂

¹⁄₂

¹⁄₈

³⁄₄

Drawer Stop
Installation 4× Scale

Illus. 15-2. Details for upper carcass.

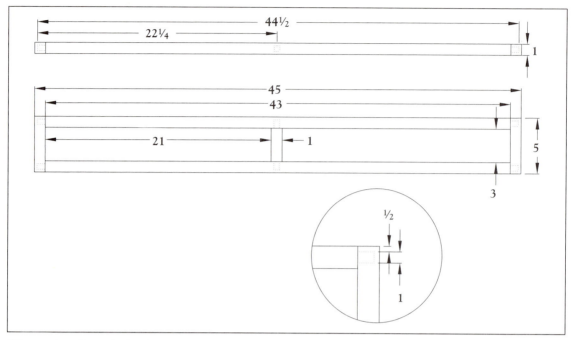

Illus. 15-3. Details for fascia.

2. Let the fascia remain longer and wider than the sides and bottom of the carcass.
3. Trim the fascia flush with the carcass on its sides and bottom.
4. Mould and cut backing boards as indicated in Illus. 15-2 and the cutting list.
5. Cut the backing boards to length to match the back of the carcass.
6. Rip the two end backing boards to width.
7. Lay the backing boards in place.
8. Set the backing boards in place with one 1½-inch finishing nail in the middle of each board located at the top, at the fixed shelfs, and at the bottom of the carcass. Do *not* glue the backing boards.
9. Trim any backing boards that extend beyond the top or bottom flush with a plane.

Building the Lower Carcass (Illus. 15-4)

1. Select panel stock that is uniform in color and grain.
2. Joint and glue up panels for the sides.

Make sure that all panels end up about ¼ inch wider and an inch or so longer than indicated in the cutting list, to allow for final trimming to size later.
3. Joint and glue up panels of secondary stock for the top.
4. Joint and glue up panels for the shelves and partition.
5. Joint and glue up a panel for the bottom.
6. Use a scraper to remove excess glue that was squeezed out when panels were clamped up.
7. Sand or plane the panels flat and level.
8. Trim the panels to size as indicated in the cutting list.
9. Mark the panels with chalk to identify which face you will want to use on the outside of the carcass. Put the best face out on the sides and up on the bottom.
10. Cut rabbets for the back of the sides, top, and bottom as indicated in Illus. 15-4 and the cutting list.
11. Bore ¼-inch-deep holes for support pins for the adjustable shelves as indicated in the drawings. Be sure to locate the holes

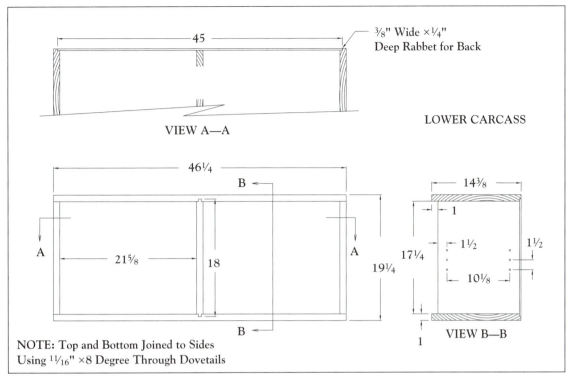

Illus. 15-4. Details for lower carcass.

accurately, so the shelves will not "rock" when they are installed.

12. Cut half-blind dovetails to join the top and bottom to the sides.
13. Cut sliding dovetails in the top and bottom panels to install the partition.
14. Scrape or sand (to 180 grit) the inside faces of the top, bottom, and partition before assembling them. Be careful to keep the panels level and flat.
15. Assemble the top and bottom to the sides.
16. Check the carcass for square by taking diagonal measurements.
17. If necessary, go ahead and cut the plywood back and set it in the back rabbets to hold it square while glue cures.

Gluing the Partition in Place

1. Apply glue only to the front two to three inches of dovetail joint and wipe off the excess glue with a damp sponge.
2. Cut the facing strips about $\frac{1}{16}$ inch longer than the carcass is wide.
3. Glue and clamp the facing strips into place.
4. Plane or sand the facing strips flush with top and bottom panels and with sides.
5. Cut a piece of $\frac{1}{4}$-inch-thick knotty pine plywood for the back.
6. Install the plywood back with 1 -inch brads and glue. Remember to wipe excess glue from inside the carcass with a damp sponge.

Building the Upper Doors (Illus. 15-5)

1. Select stock that is uniform in color and grain.
2. Cut the stiles and rails as indicated in the cutting list.

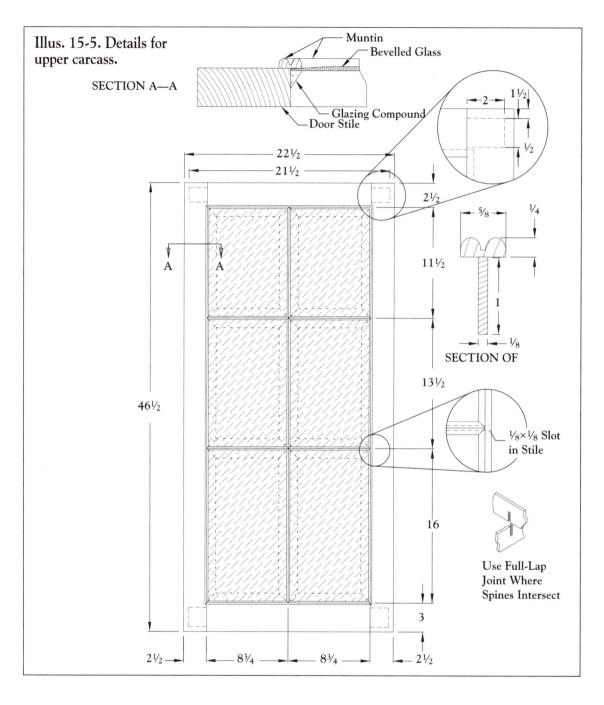

Illus. 15-5. Details for upper carcass.

SECTION A—A

Muntin
Bevelled Glass
Glazing Compound
Door Stile

SECTION OF

1/8 × 1/8 Slot in Stile

Use Full-Lap Joint Where Spines Intersect

3. Cut 1/8-inch-wide slots in the stiles and rails to set glass spines in. Cut the top and bottom rails at the same time with the stock clamped together, to ensure alignment. Use the same process to cut the slots for the stiles.

4. Cut the tenons on the rails.
5. Use the tenons to mark the mortise locations.
6. Cut the mortises.
7. Assemble and pin the mortise-and-tenon joints. First, install the pins from the

interior side of the door. Use glue. Then wipe off the excess glue with a damp sponge. Next, cut the pins flush with a flush-trimming saw. Then smooth the pins with a plane or scraper after the glue has cured. Resist the temptation to use a belt sander because a simple slip could ruin the door frame beyond repair.

8. Smooth the joint line where the stiles and rails meet by sanding or by using a cabinet scraper or plane.
9. Use a bench plane to trim the doors for proper fit with the carcass.
10. Mark and prepare mortises for the butt hinges. Align the top of the upper hinge with the bottom edge of the top rail, and the bottom of the lower hinge with the top edge of the bottom rail.
11. Install the hinges with *one* screw per leaf.
12. Check the door operation and its final fit with the carcass.
13. Remove the hinges.
14. Drill any mounting holes needed for door pulls or bullet catches.
15. Cut the $1/8$-inch-thick ×1-inch-wide

glass spines to fit in the slots cut earlier. Use scrap stock.

16. Cut moulding in the muntins with a scratch stock or router. Use scrap stock. Work on the edge of the scrap board and then trim the moulding off. This is safer and easier than working with the smaller stock.
17. Cut the muntins to fit the doors. Use a mitre bench hook for final trimming of mitred joints.
18. Glue and clamp the muntins in place.

Building the Joining Frame (Illus. 15-6)

1. Cut front and side rails one inch longer and $1/32$ inch wider than indicated in the cutting list.
2. Cut the ogee moulding.
3. Cut the groove.
4. Cut the rabbet.
5. Cut a mitre on one end of each frame member. Pay attention to the mitre-cut

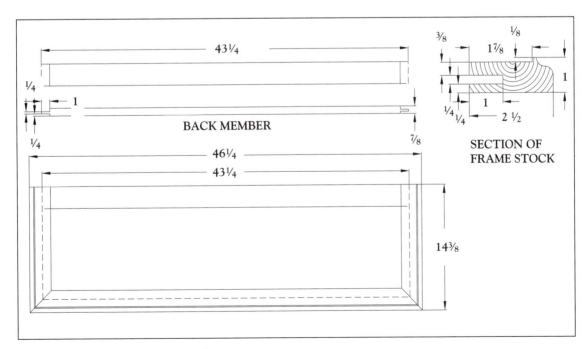

Illus. 15-6. Details for joining frame.

direction! Remember that the mitres have to meet at the corners.

6. Use the carcass to mark the front frame member for the second mitre cut.
7. Temporarily mount the front frame member to the upper carcass with one screw in the middle.
8. Use the carcass to mark the side members for length.
9. Cut the side members to length.
10. Cut the back rail to fit the spacing of the side frame members at the back of the frame. Be sure to allow extra length for the tenons.
11. Cut the tenons on the back frame member.
12. Mark and prepare the mortises on the side frame members.
13. Cut some secondary stock to fit in the grooves.
14. Assemble the mortise-and-tenon joints.
15. Assemble the front mitre joints and reinforce them by gluing filler material in the groove at the inside corner of the joint.
16. Temporarily attach the joining frame to the upper carcass. Use the same screw you used earlier plus one on the back rail.
17. Set the upper carcass/joining frame assembly on the lower carcass. Make sure it is centered in position with the joining frame flush or extending slightly more than the lower carcass. Hold the assemblies in place with a couple of C-clamps, being sure to use small blocks of wood to avoid marring the project.
18. Drive a couple of screws up through the top of the lower carcass into the front member of the joining frame.
19. Remove the C-clamps.
20. Use a block plane to trim the frame members flush with the lower carcass.

Be careful to work the plane towards the middle of the frame members at the mitred corners. Set the plane for *very light* cuts. After the frame is flush with the carcass, use the plane to dress up the curve of the ogee if necessary.

Building the Lower Doors (Illus. 15-7)

1. Select stock with uniform color and grain.
2. Joint and glue up the panels.
3. Mark all stock for their outside faces.
4. Cut the stiles and rails to the dimensions indicated in the cutting list.
5. Mark out and cut tenons in the rails.
6. Mark out and prepare mortises in the stiles.
7. Cut the grooves in the stiles and rails.
8. Use the cut grooves to mark and cut the haunch on the tenons.
9. Use a scraper to remove the glue that was squeezed out on the panel stock during clamp up.
10. Plane or sand the panel stock flat and level.
11. Cut the door panels to the dimensions indicated in the cutting list.
12. Raise the door panels with a panel-raising plane, shaper, table saw, or router.
13. Prepare the raised panel and frame parts for finishing before assembly. Do this by sanding, scraping, or by making *very light* passes with a plane. Be careful to keep the internal surfaces of the frame straight and square, especially where they meet.
14. Assemble the doors.
15. Smooth the joint line where the stiles and rails meet by sanding or using a cabinet scraper or plane.
16. Peg the mortise-and-tenon joints with $\frac{1}{4}$-inch dowel stock.
17. Wipe the excess glue off the pins with a damp sponge.
18. Cut the pins flush and dress them up with a plane or scraper.
19. Check the height fit of the doors in the carcass. Make light cuts with a bench plane on the top and bottom of the doors until the fit is achieved. Make all passes over the end grain of the stiles towards the rail, to avoid tear-out. Try to take an equal amount from top and bottom to keep the panel centered on the finished doors.

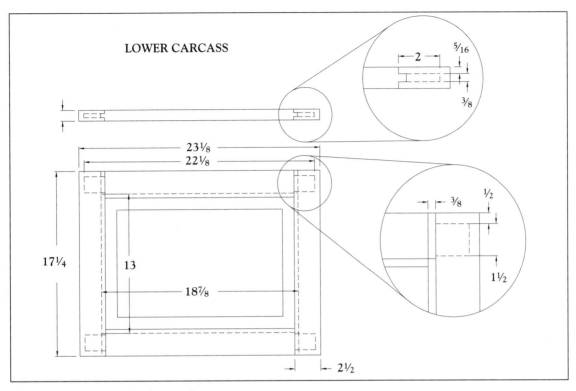

Illus. 15-7. Details for lower doors.

20. Mark out and prepare the hinge mortises.
21. Hang the doors using only one screw per hinge leaf. Make sure that the hinge stile is flush with the side of the carcass.
22. Make light passes with a plane on the lock stiles until a good fit is made between the doors. Try to take an equal number of passes on each door, to keep the joint line centered on the carcass.
23. Remove the doors from the carcass.
24. Drill any hardware holes such as for door pulls or bullet catches.

Making the Base Frame/Bracket feet (Illus. 15-8–15-10)

1. Cut the front and side rails 1 inch longer and $\frac{1}{32}$ inch wider than indicated in the cutting list.
2. Cut the ogee moulding.
3. Cut the groove.
4. Cut the rabbet.
5. Cut a mitre on one end of each frame member. Pay attention to the mitre cut direction! Remember that the mitres have to meet at the corners.
6. Use the carcass to mark the front frame member for a second mitre cut.
7. Temporarily mount the front frame member to the upper carcass with one screw in the middle of the upper carcass.
8. Use the carcass to mark the side members for length.
9. Cut the side members to length.
10. Cut the back rail to fit the spacing of the side frame members at the back of the frame. Be sure to allow extra length for the tenons.
11. Cut the tenons on the back frame member.
12. Mark and prepare the mortises on the side frame members.

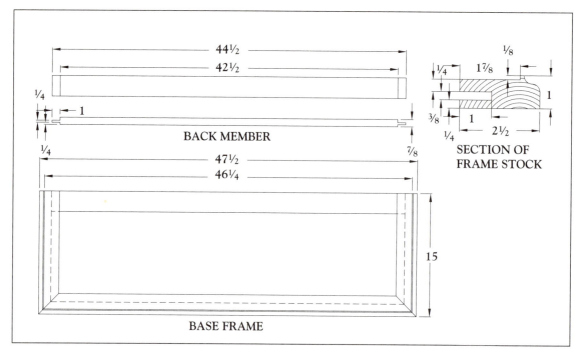

44½

42½

¼

1

BACK MEMBER

⅛
¼   1⅞
1
⅜   1
¼   2½

SECTION OF
FRAME STOCK

¼   47½   ⅞
46¼

15

BASE FRAME

Illus. 15-8. Details for base frame.

13. Cut some secondary stock to fit in the grooves. (Secondary stock is less-expensive stock used in the parts of the project that are not in view.)
14. Assemble the mortise-and-tenon joints.
15. Assemble the front mitre joints and reinforce them by gluing filler material in the groove at the inside corner of the joint.
16. Cut the stock for the front and back foot brackets at the dimensions indicated in the cutting list.
17. Cut the stock for the side feet to match the length of the side member of the base frame.
18. Lay out the shape of the front bracket feet on one blank. The pattern should be aligned with the top of the board, and the board should be wide enough to accommodate the layout of the radii of the various curves.
19. Cut one front foot blank to shape.
20. Use the foot you just cut to transfer the pattern to the other blank.

21. Cut the other foot to shape.
22. Cut the stock for the side feet to match the length of the side member of the base frame.
23. Lay out the shape of the side bracket feet on one blank. The pattern should be aligned with the top of the board, and the board should be wide enough to accommodate the layout of the radii of the various curves.
24. Cut one side foot blank to shape.
25. Use the foot you just cut to transfer the pattern to the other blank.
26. Cut the other foot to shape.
27. Rip the feet to width. They must be consistent in width. If you're using a table saw, cut them all at the same rip fence setting.
28. Joint the top edge of the bracket feet for a clean joint with the base frame.
29. Join the front bracket feet to the side feet with through dovetails. Make sure that they are square.

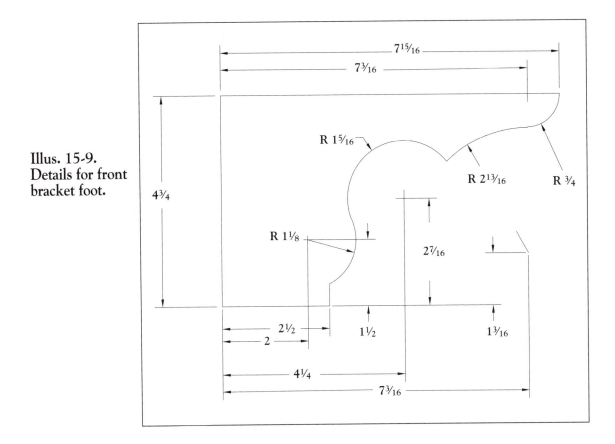

Illus. 15-9.
Details for front
bracket foot.

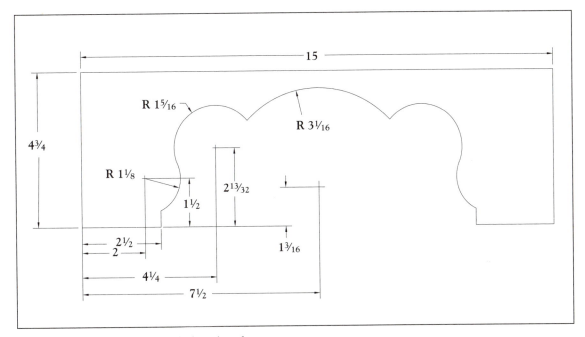

Illus. 15-10. Details for side bracket foot.

30. Join the back foot brackets to the side feet with half-blind dovetails. Make sure that they are square.
31. Edge-glue and clamp the bracket feet onto the base frame.
32. Using a block plane, take *light cuts* and dress the base frame down to match with the bracket feet. If necessary, dress over the curve on the ogee. Remember to make cuts over the mitre joints from the "outside" in.

Making the Drawers (Illus. 15-11)

1. Cut the fronts slightly larger than the opening in the fascia.
2. Rip the sides of pine to match the height of the opening in the fascia.
3. Cut the sides about an inch longer than indicated in the cutting list.
4. Trim the fronts to match the opening in the fascia.
5. Cut half-blind dovetails to join the sides to the fronts. Do not glue them yet. Cut a ¼-inch-wide × ¼-inch-deep dado in the middle of the bottom dovetail.
6. Dry-join the fronts to the sides.
7. Insert the drawers into their openings with their fronts going into the carcass.
8. Mark the sides of the drawers flush with the front of the fascia.
9. Mark the drawers and drawer parts to identify the left and right drawers.
10. Disassemble the dovetail joints and cut

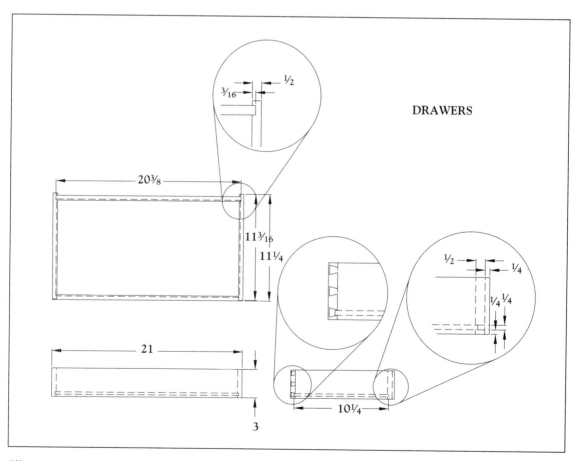

Illus. 15-11. Details for drawers.

the sides to the length you just marked.

11. Cut a dado on the back of the drawer sides as indicated in Illus.15-11.
12. Cut the drawer bottoms from ¼-inch knotty pine plywood. They should be ⅛ inch narrower than the distance between the dado bottoms, and long enough to align with the back edge of the dadoes you cut on the sides so you can attach the drawer back.
13. Cut the back of the drawer to fit in the dadoes in the sides.
14. Rip the back of the drawer to sit on top of the drawer bottom and flush with the top of the sides.
15. Prepare the inside surfaces of the drawer parts for finishing.
16. Glue and assemble the dovetail joints.
17. Slide the drawer bottom into place.
18. Glue the drawer back in place.
19. Drill any holes for drawer pulls.

Making the Pediment (Illus. 15-12 and 15-13)

1. Cut the front and side rails 1 inch longer and ¹⁄₃₂ inch wider than indicated in the cutting-list.
2. Cut the ogee moulding.
3. Cut the groove.
4. Cut the rabbet.
5. Cut a mitre on one end of each frame

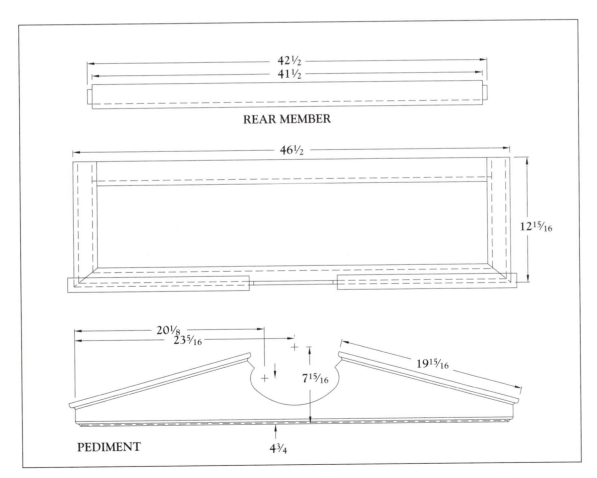

Illus. 15-12. Details for pediment.

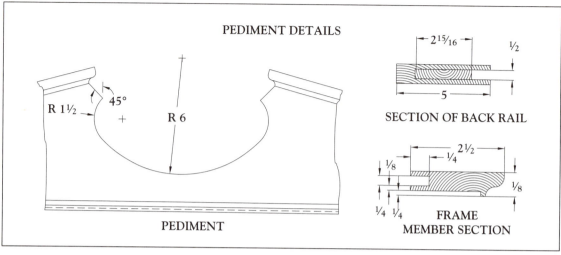

Illus. 15-13. Details for pediment.

member. Pay attention to the mitre cut direction! Remember that the mitres have to meet at the corners.

6. Use the carcass to mark the front frame member for a second mitre cut.
7. Temporarily mount the front frame member to the upper carcass with one screw in the middle of the upper carcass.
8. Use the carcass to mark the side members for length.
9. Cut the side members to length.
10. Cut the back rail to fit the spacing on the back of the side frame members. Be sure to allow extra length for the tenons.
11. Cut the tenons on the back frame member.
12. Mark and prepare the mortises on the side frame members.
13. Cut some secondary stock to fit in the grooves.
14. Assemble the mortise-and-tenon joints.
15. Assemble the front mitre joints and reinforce them by gluing a filler material in the groove at the inside corner of the joint.
16. Temporarily attach the frame to the upper carcass. Use the same screw you used earlier plus one on the back rail.
17. Cut the pediment board to the dimen-

sions indicated in the cutting list.
18. Lay out the shape of the pediment on a piece of poster board and cut the shape out with a sharp knife.
19. Transfer the pattern to the pediment stock by tracing the poster-board template.
20. Cut the pattern out.
21. Smooth any saw marks in the oval area with a half-round wood rasp, followed by a finer half-round file.
22. Joint the sloped edges.
23. Cut the top moulding boards to the dimensions indicated in the cutting list and form the ogee on all four edges.
24. Joint the bottom of the moulding boards.
25. Edge-glue the moulding boards onto the sloped edges of the pediment board.
26. Edge-glue the pediment board to the frame assembly. Align it with the top front edge and the sides of the frame.

Finish

1. Disassemble the doors and frames from the carcasss.
2. Sand all surfaces with sandpaper in progression down to 220 grit, or use a finely set cabinet scraper to smooth the surface.

3. Apply sanding sealer consisting of one-part gloss polyurethane to two parts mineral spirits to all surfaces.
4. Sand the surfaces with 280-grit open-coat sandpaper.
5. Wipe all parts with tack cloth.
6. Apply a coat of gloss polyurethane to all surfaces. Work on horizontal surfaces to avoid runs and sags. After the finish has begun to cure, rotate the parts to turn the other surfaces horizantal. Allow 24 hours of cure time.
7. Sand all surfaces with 320-grit wet/dry cloth lubricated with soapy water until the surface is flat and free of dust nibs, etc.
8. Wipe all surfaces with a sponge wet with clear, clean water. Be sure to remove *all* sanding residue.
9. Apply a second coat of gloss polyurethane to all surfaces. Work on horizontal surfaces to avoid runs and sags. After the finish has begun to cure, rotate the parts to turn another surface horizontal. Allow 24 hours of cure time.
10. Sand all surfaces with 380-grit wet/dry cloth lubricated with soapy water until the surface is flat and free of dust nibs, etc.
11. Wipe all surfaces with a wet sponge using clear, clean water. Be sure to remove *all* sanding residue.
12. Apply a third coat of gloss polyurethane to all surfaces. Work on horizontal surfaces to avoid runs and sags. After the finish has begun to cure, rotate the parts to turn another surface horizontal. Allow 24 hours of cure time.
13. Sand all surfaces with 600-grit wet/dry cloth lubricated with soapy water until the "glaze" is removed.
14. Wipe all surfaces with a wet sponge using clear, clean water. Be sure to remove *all* sanding residue.
15. Rub all surfaces with rottenstone powder lubricated with paraffin oil until a uniform gloss is achieved.
16. Clean all rottenstone and paraffin oil residue from the finish.

Assembling the Parts

1. Mount the joining frame onto the upper carcass. To do this, screw the front member to the carcass bottom using four countersunk, flathead screws. Then screw the side members to the carcass bottom with three screws each. Use slotted, countersunk holes for the back and mid-span screws.
2. Attach the lower carcass to the joining frame. Start with the same screw holes used earlier for alignment. Use slotted holes in the lower carcass for screws going into the side frame parts.
3. Install the base frame on the lower carcass.
4. Mount the pediment frame on the upper carcass.
5. Install door pulls and other hardware.
6. Install drawer pulls on the drawers.
7. Install doors on the lower carcass.
8. Glaze the upper carcass doors.
9. Attach the doors to the upper carcass.
10. Install the drawers.
11. Move the completed bookcase into position.
12. Apply a coat of furniture polish.
13. Put in the shelf pins and adjustable shelves.
14. Enjoy! ◙

Cutting List page 142

Bill of Materials page 145

Table 15-1. Cutting list for the bookcase.

CUTTING LIST

Item Number	Part Name	Quantity	Material	Thickness (inches)	Width (inches)	Length (inches)	Note
1	Upper Carcass Top	1	Primary Wood	1	13 ½	45	
2	Upper Carcass Sides	2	Primary Wood	1	12½	54½	
3	Upper Carcass Partition	1	Primary Wood	1	12	53¼	1
4	Upper Carcass Fixed Shelf	2	Primary Wood	1	12	21¾	1
5	Upper Carcass Door Bottom Rail	2	Primary Wood	1	3	29½	2, 3
6	Upper Carcass Door Top Rail	2	Primary Wood	1	2½	29½	2, 3
7	Upper Carcass Door Stile	4	Primary Wood	1	2½	46½	3
8	Fascia Top Rail	1	Primary Wood	1	1	44½	3
9	Fascia Bottom Rail	1	Primary Wood	1	1	44½	3
10	Fascia Stile	2	Primary Wood	1	1	5⅛	
11	Fascia Partition	1	Primary Wood	1	1	4 ½	
12	Joining Frame Front	1	Primary Wood	1	2½	46½	1, 3

Cutting List (continued)

Item Number	Part Name	Quantity	Material	Thickness (inches)	Width (inches)	Length (inches)	Note
13	Joining Frame Side	2	Primary Wood	1	$2\frac{1}{2}$	$20\frac{3}{8}$	1, 3
14	Lower Carcass Top/Bottom	2	Primary Wood	1	$14\frac{3}{8}$	$46\frac{1}{4}$	
15	Lower Carcass Side	2	Primary Wood	1	$13\frac{3}{8}$	$19\frac{1}{4}$	
16	Lower Carcass Partition	1	Primary Wood	1	13	18	1
17	Lower Carcass Door Rail	4	Primary Wood	1	$2\frac{1}{2}$	$22\frac{1}{8}$	3
18	Lower Carcass Door Stile	4	Primary Wood	1	$2\frac{1}{2}$	$17\frac{1}{4}$	2, 3
19	Base Frame Front	1	Primary Wood	1	$2\frac{1}{2}$	$47\frac{1}{2}$	1, 3
20	Base Frame Sides	2	Primary Wood	1	$2\frac{1}{2}$	15	1, 3
21	Front Foot Blank	6	Primary Wood	1	$4\frac{3}{4}$	$7\frac{15}{16}$	4
22	Side Foot Blank	2	Primary Wood	1	$4\frac{3}{4}$	15	
23	Pediment Frame Front	1	Primary Wood	1	$2\frac{1}{2}$	$46\frac{1}{2}$	1, 3
24	Pediment Frame Side	2	Primary Wood	1	$2\frac{1}{2}$	$18\frac{15}{16}$	1, 3
25	Carcass Door Panel		Primary Wood	$3/4$	$18\frac{7}{8}$	$18\frac{3}{4}$	3
26	Upper Carcass Floating Shelf	4	Primary Wood	$3/4$	12	21	1

Cutting List (continued)

Item Number	Part Name	Quantity	Material	Thickness (inches)	Width (inches)	Length (inches)	Note
27	Pediment Top Rail	2	Primary Wood	$3/4$	$1\frac{1}{2}$	$19\frac{15}{16}$	1
28	Drawer Front	2	Primary Wood	$1/2$	3	21	1
29	Pediment Board	1	Primary Wood	$1/2$	8	$46\frac{1}{2}$	
30	Upper Carcass Backing Board	17	Primary Wood	$1/2$	3	$54\frac{1}{2}$	1
31	Vertical Glass Spine	2	Primary Wood	$1/8$	1	$41\frac{3}{4}$	6
32	Horizontal Glass Spine	4	Primary Wood	$1/8$	1	$18\frac{3}{4}$	6
33	Back Foot	2	Secondary Wood	$7/8$	$4\frac{3}{4}$	$7\frac{15}{16}$	
34	Upper Carcass Bottom	1	Secondary Wood	$7/8$	12	45	
35	Joining Frame Back Rail	1	Secondary Wood	$7/8$	$2\frac{1}{2}$	$43\frac{1}{4}$	
36	Base Frame Back Rail	1	Secondary Wood	$7/8$	$2\frac{1}{2}$	$44\frac{1}{2}$	
37	Pediment Frame Back Rail	1	Secondary Wood	$7/8$	$2\frac{1}{2}$	$42\frac{1}{2}$	
38	Drawer Side	4	Secondary Wood	$1/2$	3	$9\frac{1}{2}$	1
39	Drawer Back	2	Secondary Wood	$1/2$	3	$20\frac{3}{8}$	1
40	Drawer Stop	2	Secondary Wood	$1/2$	$5/8$	$20\frac{3}{8}$	1
41	Drawer Bottom	2	Plywood	$1/4$	$20\frac{1}{4}$	$10\frac{1}{4}$	5

Cutting List (continued)

Item Number	Part Name	Quantity	Material	Thickness (inches)	Width (inches)	Length (inches)	Note
42	Lower Carcass Back	1	Plywood	$\frac{1}{4}$	18 $\frac{1}{4}$	44	1
43	Upper Glass Pane	4		$\frac{3}{32}$	8$\frac{5}{8}$	11$\frac{3}{8}$	6
44	Mid-level Glass Pane	4		$\frac{3}{32}$	8$\frac{5}{8}$	13 3/8	6
45	Lower Glass Pane	4		$\frac{3}{32}$	8$\frac{5}{8}$	15 $\frac{7}{8}$	6

NOTES:

1. Cut part to match carcass.
2. Cut $\frac{1}{8}$ inch longer and then trim to fit carcass on assembly.
3. Cut $\frac{1}{16}$ inch wider and then trim to fit carcass on assembly.
4. Cut 1 inch wider and longer, and then form.
5. Cut to match drawer.
6. Cut to match the doors.

Table 14-2. Bill of materials.

BILL OF MATERIALS

Item Number	Description	Quantity	Vendor	Unit Cost	Total Cost
1	$\frac{5}{4}$ Black walnut S2S to 1 inch	78			
2	$\frac{4}{4}$ Black walnut S2S to $\frac{3}{4}$ inch	12			
3	$\frac{4}{4}$ Black walnut S2S to $\frac{1}{2}$ inch	34			
4	$\frac{4}{4}$ D-grade select pine S2S to $\frac{7}{8}$ inch	11			

Bill of Materials (continued)

Item Number	Description	Quantity	Vendor	Unit Cost	Total Cost
5	$4/4$ D-grade select pine S2S to $1/2$ inch	5			
6	sheet of $1/4$-inch knotty pine plywood	1			
7	$3/32$-inch bevelled glass cut to fit upper carcass doors	12			
8	door pulls	4			
9	$3/4$-inch cast brass drawer pull knobs	4			
10	brass hinge pairs with screws	4			
11	$3/8$-inch bullet catches	4			
12	quart of slow-set yellow woodworker's glue	1			
13	$1 1/2$-inch finishing nails	$1/4$ pound			
14	1-inch finishing nails	$1/4$ pound			
15	$1 1/4$-inch flathead #8 wood screws	30			
16	high-gloss polyurethane	2 quarts			
17	mineral spirits	1 gallon			
18	320-grit wet/dry sandpaper	5 sheets			
19	360-grit wet/dry sandpaper	5 sheets			
20	canister of rottenstone	1 pound			
21	paraffin oil	1 pint			

16 BUILDING A TOOL CHEST

Every furniture craftsman needs a place in his shop to store his tools. The tool chest shown in Illus. 16-1 is intended to do just that. It's been designed to handle just about all of your hand tools. If you would like to, you could design and build a base cabinet to take care of your portable power tools.

Following is a project file for building a tool chest. It includes a bill of materials, cutting list, construction instructions, and drawings. This type of project file is what I strongly recommend for all projects.

Illus. 16-1. Tool chest.

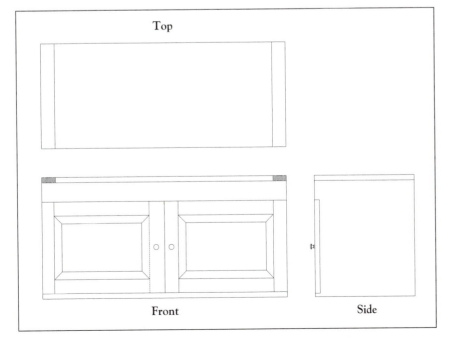

147

CONSTRUCTION INSTRUCTIONS

Panel Preparation

1. Joint stock and glue up ¾-inch-thick panels for the top, bottom, and sides of the carcass. Be sure to make the panels slightly longer and wider than needed for final trimming to size.
2. Plane or sand the panels smooth and flat.
3. Joint stock and glue up a ¾-inch-thick panel for the tray bottom. Be sure to leave the panels slightly longer and wider than needed for final trimming to size.
4. Plane or sand the panel smooth and flat.

Making the Drawer Frames (Illus. 16-2–16-6)

1. Cut the drawer frame sides to length with a table saw. Use a stop block on the mitre gauge to ensure uniformity. Allow for the tenons on the ends.
2. Cut the intermediate drawer-frame runners to the same length as the drawer-frame sides.
3. Rip the drawer-frame sides to width.
4. Cut the drawer-frame fronts and backs to length. Make sure they are all uniform.
5. Rip the drawer-frame fronts and backs to ¼ inch greater than the width indicated in the cutting list.

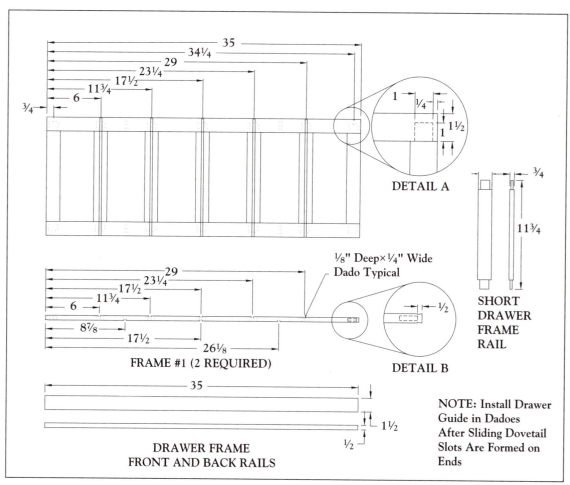

Illus. 16-2. Details for drawer frame partition #1.

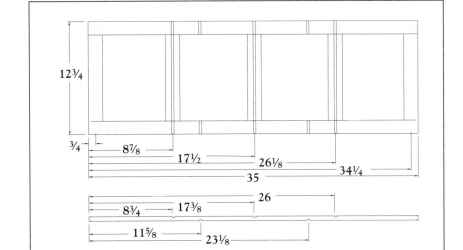

Illus. 16-3. Details for drawer frame partition # 2.

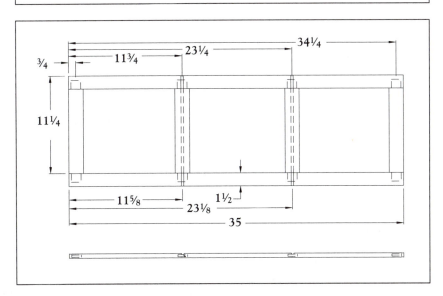

Illus. 16-4. Details for drawer frame partition # 3.

Illus. 16-5. Details for drawer frame partition # 4.

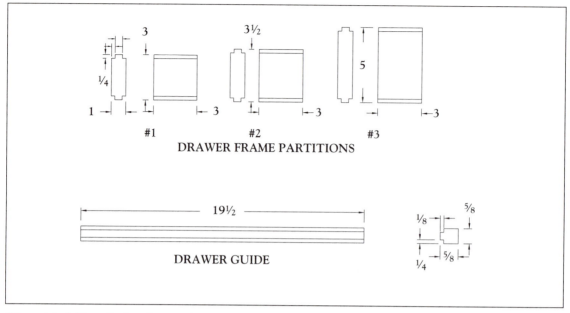

Illus. 16-6. Details for drawer frame partitions and drawer guide.

6. Prepare mortises in the front and back drawer-frame members.
7. Form tenons on the drawer-frame sides and the intermediate runners.
8. Assemble the drawer frames.
9. Plane, scrape, or sand the assembled frames to eliminate gaps or bumps where the parts come together.
10. Trim the drawer frames and tray bottom to uniform lengths.
11. Cut dadoes for the drawer guides.
12. Cut the drawer guides to fit the dadoes.
13. Cut the drawer guides to length and glue them in place.

Making the Back (Illus. 16-7)

1. Cut the top rail for the back, so the back will fit the carcass.
2. Cut the rabbet for the backing boards.
3. Install the rail into the carcass assembly.
4. Cut the backing boards to shape, and then cut them to their lengths to fit the carcass.
5. Install the backing boards with finish nails.

Making the Fascia (Illus. 16-8)

1. Cut the fascia panel and end caps. The fascia panel should be cut a little wide for final trimming with a plane after installation.
2. Cut mortises in the fascia panel and assemble it with the end caps.
3. Glue up the fascia assembly.
4. Plane, scrape, or sand the fascia smooth and flat.
5. Prepare a mortise in the top edge of the fascia for a chest lock. Make sure it is a little deep, to allow the lock to sit properly after the fascia has been trimmed and installed.

Carcass Assembly (Illus. 16-9–16-13)

1. Trim the side panels to their finished sizes.
2. Cut the rabbet on the back of the side panels.
3. Cut sliding dovetail slots in the side panels.

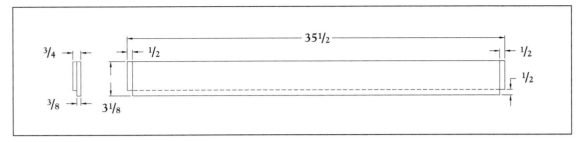

Illus. 16-7. Details for back rail.

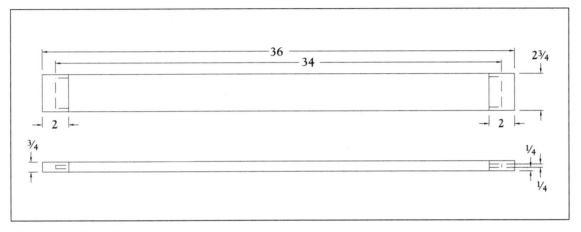

Illus. 16-8. Details for fascia.

4. Cut dovetails on the ends of the drawer frames and tray bottom.
5. Cut the bottom panel to width.
6. Cut half-blind dovetail pins on the inside bottom edge of the side panels.
7. Trim the drawer frames and tray bottom to final width.
8. Dry assemble the drawer frames, sides, and tray. Make sure all the parts are flush with or extend slightly at the front of the carcass sides. They can be trimmed with a plane after assembly, if required. The forward edge of the tray bottom must be flush with the carcass sides, and straight.
9. Cut the bottom panel to length. Mark the panel with the side panels.
10. Cut the dovetails on the bottom panel to fit the side panels.
11. Glue up the bottom and side panels.
12. Glue the tray bottom in place.
13. Glue the drawer frames in place.
14. Use a plane to trim the tray bottom and drawer frames flush with the carcass sides.
15. Smooth the dovetail joinery on the bottom panel by planing, scraping, or sanding.
16. Cut the drawer partitions to length by matching the spacing on the drawer frames.
17. Cut the tongue on the drawer partitions.
18. Install the drawer partitions.
19. Trim the drawer partitions flush with the drawer frames by planing or scraping.
20. Trim the back boards to final size to match the carcass.
21. Joint the bottom edge of the fascia.
22. Glue the fascia in place. Make sure that the jointed edge aligns with the tray bottom.
23. Use a plane to trim the fascia to match the carcass.

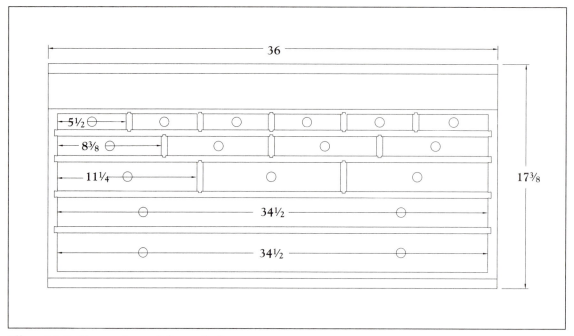

Illus. 16-9. Front view of the tool chest.

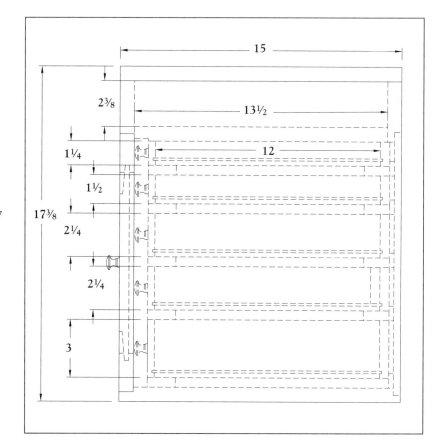

Illus. 16-10. Side view
of the tool chest.

Making the Drawers (Illus. 16-14)

1. Rip the drawer fronts, backs, and sides to match the openings in the carcass.
2. Cut the drawer fronts and backs to lengths that match the openings in the carcass. Mark the parts for matching fronts and backs.
3. Prepare the groove for the drawer bottoms.
4. Cut joints to assemble the drawer fronts, sides, and backs.
5. Cut ¼-inch-thick plywood drawer bottoms. Leave them ¹⁄₁₆ inch longer and wider than indicated in the cutting list, to allow the panel to float.
6. Mark the middle of each drawer front for hardware installation.
7. Assemble the drawers.

Making the Top (Illus. 16-15)

1. Cut the top panel to the length indicated in the cutting list and ⅛ inch wider.

Use the carcass-assembly measurements.
2. Cut the breadboard ends to the widths indicated in the cutting list and ⅛ inch longer. Use the carcass assembly measurements.
3. Cut the tenons on the panel.
4. Mark the breadboard ends for mortises to match the tenons.
5. Prepare the mortises.
6. Attach the breadboard ends to the panel. Peg every other tenon into its mortise, starting at the middle tenon and going out.
7. Install the pegs from the bottom of the joint.
8. Level and smooth the top by planing, scraping, or sanding it.

Making the Doors (Illus. 16-16)

1. Joint and glue up stock for the door panels.
2. Smooth and flatten the panels by planing or sanding them.

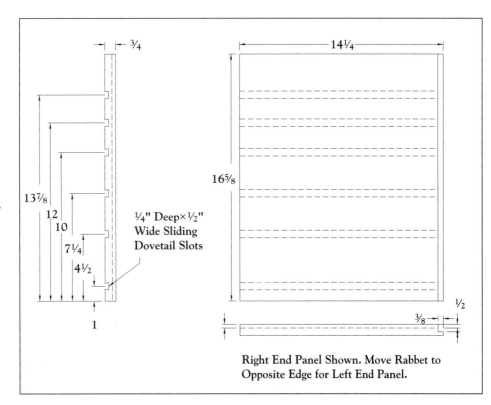

Illus. 16-11. Details for side panels.

¾

13⅞
12
10
7¼
4½
1

¼" Deep × ½" Wide Sliding Dovetail Slots

14¼

16⅝

½

⅜

Right End Panel Shown. Move Rabbet to Opposite Edge for Left End Panel.

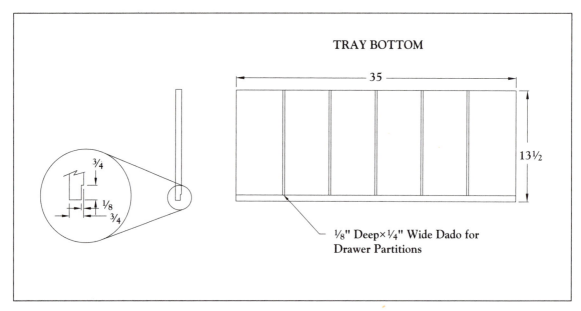

Illus. 16-12. Details for tray bottom.

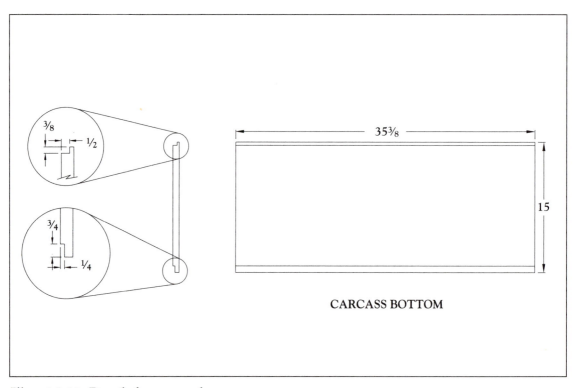

Illus. 16-13. Details for carcass bottom.

3. Rip the stiles and rails to $\frac{1}{16}$ inch wider than indicated in the cutting list.
4. Cut the stiles to $\frac{1}{16}$ inch longer than indicated in the cutting list.
5. Cut the rails to length.
6. Cut the groove for the door panel.
7. Prepare the mortises.
8. Cut the haunched tenons. Size the haunch to fit the groove you already cut.
9. Cut the door panels to size.
10. Raise the door panels.
11. Prepare the door panels for finishing *before* fitting them into the frames by sanding, planing, or scraping them.
12. Smooth the inside edges of the frame parts before assembly by planing, scraping, or sanding them. If you sand, be careful to leave the surface flat and straight.
13. Prepare a lock mortise on the right upper stile.
14. Assemble the doors. Pin the mortise-and-tenons with two $\frac{1}{4}$-inch dowels at each joint. Do *not* glue the panel in place.
15. Make the door frames smooth by planing or sanding them.

Final Assembly

1. Lay the top in place and mark the hinge locations.
2. Cut mortises in the top and on the back frame upper rail for the hinges.
3. Install the hinges with only one screw per leaf.
4. Use a block or smoothing plane to final-trim the top to fit the carcass.

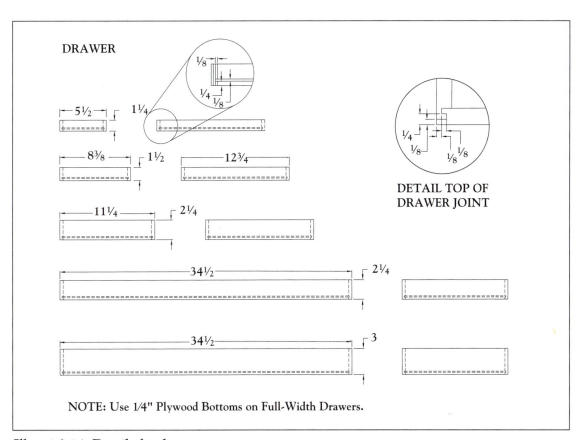

Illus. 16-14. Details for drawers.

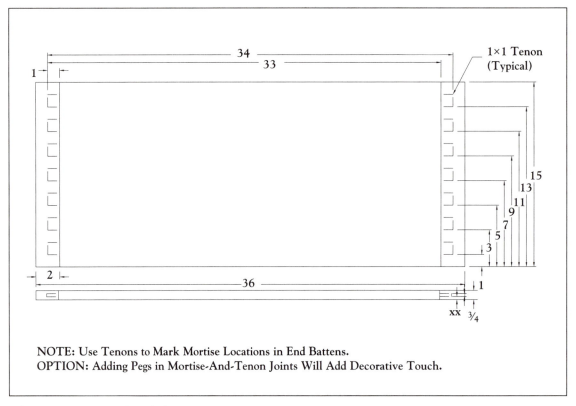

NOTE: Use Tenons to Mark Mortise Locations in End Battens.
OPTION: Adding Pegs in Mortise-And-Tenon Joints Will Add Decorative Touch.

Illus. 16-15. Top of tool chest.

5. Remove the hinges.
6. Cut moulding on the top edges on the front and sides.
7. Mark the top for a mortise that matches the lock mortise on the fascia.
8. Cut the lock mortise in the top and fit the mortise in the fascia to fit the lock body. Do *not* install the lock permanently until after finishing the chest.
9. Set the doors in position.
10. Trim the doors with a plane until they fit their openings with about a $1/32$-inch gap on their tops and bottoms.
11. Trim the lock stiles on the doors until they fit together with $1/32$-inch clearance.
12. Mark and cut the hinge mortises.
13. Install the hinges with one screw per leaf and check their fit. Trim the hinges with a block plane as required.
14. Mark and cut a mortise in the bottom of the

fascia to match the lock mortise in the door.
15. Remove the hinges.

Finishing

1. Smooth all exterior surfaces by scraping or sanding them. If sanding, use up to 180-grit sandpaper.
2. Sand and install the wooden drawer pulls.
3. Sand and install the wooden door pulls.
4. Wipe the surfaces with a moist sponge and allow them to dry.
5. Apply a grain filler to smooth the surface pores per the manufacturer's instructions.
6. Sand the surfaces with 280-grit sandpaper.
7. Apply stain or dye as wanted per the manufacturer's instructions.
8. Apply a sealer of one-part high-gloss polyurethane to three parts mineral spirits. Allow it 24 hours to cure.

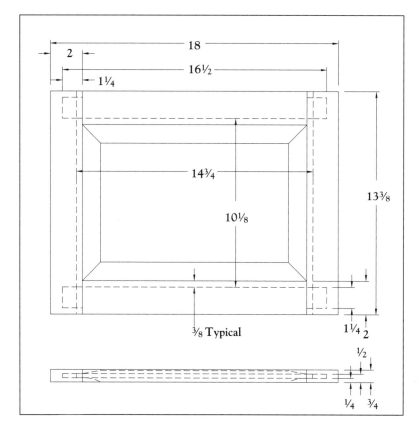

Illus. 16-16. Door detail.

9. Sand the surfaces with 320-grit sandpaper.
10. Apply a coat of high-gloss polyurethane and allow it 24 hours to cure.
11. Rub out the polyurethane with #000 steel wool or 320-grit wet/dry sandpaper lubricated with soapy water. Be sure to remove all the little imperfections from the finish.
12. Wipe the work with a tack cloth.
13. Apply a second coat of high-gloss polyurethane.
14. Rub out the polyurethane with #000 steel wool or 320-grit wet/dry sandpaper lubricated with soapy water. Be sure to remove all the little imperfections from the finish.
15. Wipe the work with a tack cloth.
16. Apply a third coat of high-gloss polyurethane.
17. Sand the surfaces with 380-grit wet/dry sandpaper lubricated with soapy water.

The surfaces should now be completely smooth with no runs or dust nibs.
18. Lightly wash the surfaces with a moist cloth or sponge. Rinse the surfaces often and allow them to dry.
19. Polish the finish with rottenstone lubricated with paraffin oil.
20. Lightly wash the surfaces with a moist cloth or sponge. Rinse them often and allow them to dry.
21. Wipe the work with furniture cleaner.
22. Be sure to give interior and exterior surfaces the same amount of finish.

Finishing Touches

1. Install the locks.
2. Install stays to keep the lid up.
3. Install the hinges on the doors.

Lining The Drawers and Top Tray

1. Cut pieces of poster board to fit in the bottoms of the drawers and the top tray. These pieces should be $\frac{1}{16}$ inch shorter and narrower than the drawers and the top tray.
2. Cut fabric to fit the poster board and exceed one inch past the edges of the poster board.
3. Coat the back of the fabric with spray adhesive. Be careful not to use too much or it will soak through the fabric.
4. Center the poster board on the fabric.
5. Rub the back of the poster board for a good bond.
6. Fold the fabric over the edges of the poster board and rub it smooth.
7. Trim the raised areas of the fabric on the back of the poster board with a single-edged razor.
8. Apply the spray adhesive to the back of the fabric-covered poster board and install it in the drawer bottoms.

Tool Holders

1. Use scrap pieces of primary wood to make holders for the tools. This will prevent them from rattling around when you open or close the drawers. Make dividers to keep chisels and carving tools from rolling into each other and damaging their edges.
2. Finish the tool holders with the same stain/dye used on the tool chest and add Danish oil.
3. Install the tool holders by driving a screw from the bottom of the drawer. ◘

Table 16-1. Cutting list for the tool chest.

CUTTING LIST

Item Number	Part Name	Quantity	Material	Thickness (inches)	Width (inches)	Length (inches)	Note
1	Top Panel	1	Primary Wood	¾	15	34	
2	Breadboard End Cap	2	Primary Wood	¾	2	15	
3	Side	2	Primary Wood	¾	14¼	14⅝	
4	Bottom	1	Primary Wood	¾	15	35⅜	1
5	Tray Bottom	1	Primary Wood	¾	13½	35	
6	Door Panel	2	Primary Wood	¾	14⅝	$9\frac{15}{16}$	
7	Hinge Stile	2	Primary Wood	¾	2	13⅛	
8	Door Frame Rail	4	Primary Wood	¾	2	16½	
9	Left Lock Stile	1	Primary Wood	¾	2¼	13⅛	
10	Right Lock Stile	1	Primary Wood	¾	2	13⅛	
11	Fascia Board	1	Primary Wood	¾	2¾	34	1
12	Fascia End Cap	2	Primary Wood	¾	2	2¾	
13	Back Top Rail	1	Primary Wood	¾	3⅛	34	2
14	Drawer Frame Front	5	Primary Wood	½	1½	35	

Cutting List (continued)

Item Number	Part Name	Quantity	Material	Thickness (inches)	Width (inches)	Length (inches)	Note
15	Drawer Frame Partition 1	5	Primary Wood	$\frac{1}{2}$	$1\frac{1}{2}$	$1\frac{1}{2}$	4
16	Drawer Frame Partition 2	3	Primary Wood	$\frac{1}{2}$	$1\frac{1}{2}$	$1\frac{3}{4}$	4
17	Drawer Frame Partition 3	2	Primary Wood	$\frac{1}{2}$	$1\frac{1}{2}$	$2\frac{1}{2}$	4
18	Drawer Front 1	6	Primary Wood	$\frac{3}{8}$	$1\frac{1}{4}$	$5\frac{1}{2}$	4, 5
19	Drawer Front 2	4	Primary Wood	$\frac{3}{8}$	$1\frac{1}{2}$	$6\frac{3}{8}$	4, 5
20	Drawer Front 3	3	Primary	$\frac{3}{8}$	$2\frac{1}{4}$	$11\frac{1}{4}$	4, 5
21	Drawer Front 4	1	Primary Wood	$\frac{3}{8}$	$2\frac{1}{4}$	$34\frac{1}{2}$	4, 5
22	Drawer Front 5	1	Primary Wood	$\frac{3}{8}$	3	$34\frac{1}{2}$	4, 5
23	Drawer Frame Back Rail	5	Secondary Wood	$\frac{1}{2}$	$1\frac{1}{2}$	35	4
24	Short Drawer Frame Rail	20	Secondary Wood	$\frac{1}{2}$	$1\frac{1}{2}$	$11\frac{3}{4}$	
25	Drawer Guide	10	Secondary Wood	$\frac{1}{2}$	$\frac{5}{8}$	$11\frac{3}{4}$	
26	Drawer Side 1	12	Secondary Wood	$\frac{3}{8}$	$1\frac{1}{4}$	$12\frac{1}{2}$	4, 5
27	Drawer Side 2	8	Secondary Wood	$\frac{3}{8}$	$1\frac{1}{2}$	$12\frac{1}{2}$	4, 5
28	Drawer Side 3	8	Secondary Wood	$\frac{3}{8}$	$2\frac{1}{4}$	$12\frac{1}{2}$	4, 5

Cutting List (continued)

Item Number	Part Name	Quantity	Material	Thickness (inches)	Width (inches)	Length (inches)	Note
29	Drawer Side 4	2	Secondary Wood	$\frac{3}{8}$	3	$12\frac{1}{2}$	4, 5
30	Drawer Back 1	6	Secondary Wood	$\frac{3}{8}$	$1\frac{1}{4}$	$6\frac{1}{2}$	4, 5
31	Drawer Back 2	4	Secondary Wood	$\frac{3}{8}$	$1\frac{1}{2}$	$6\frac{3}{8}$	4, 5
32	Drawer Back 3	3	Secondary Wood	$\frac{3}{8}$	$2\frac{1}{4}$	$11\frac{1}{4}$	4, 5
33	Drawer Back 4	1	Secondary Wood	$\frac{3}{8}$	$2\frac{1}{4}$	$34\frac{1}{2}$	4, 5
34	Drawer Back 5	1	Secondary Wood	$\frac{3}{8}$	3	$34\frac{1}{2}$	4, 5
35	Back Boards	As Required	Secondary Wood	$\frac{3}{8}$	3	$13\frac{5}{8}$	6
36	Drawer Bottom 1	6	Plywood	$\frac{1}{8}$	5	$12\frac{1}{4}$	
37	Drawer Bottom 2	4	Plywood	$\frac{1}{8}$	$5\frac{7}{8}$	$12\frac{1}{4}$	
38	Drawer Bottom 3	3	Plywood	$\frac{1}{8}$	$10\frac{3}{4}$	$12\frac{1}{4}$	
39	Drawer Bottom 4	2	Plywood	$\frac{1}{4}$	$12\frac{1}{4}$	34	

NOTES:

1. Length may vary more or less than $1\frac{1}{8}$ inches because of dovetails.
2. Rip $\frac{1}{32}$ inch wider and trim back frame assembly with a bench plane for installation.
3. Cut $\frac{1}{16}$ inch long and trim back frame assembly for installation.
4. Cut to fit openings left by carcass construction.
5. Rip the drawer fronts, backs, and sides at the same time.
6. Resaw from $\frac{3}{4}$-inch-thick stock.

Stock Requirements:

21 board feet of $\frac{3}{4}$-inch-thick primary wood
20 board feet of $\frac{3}{4}$-inch-thick secondary wood (select D-grade pine)
1 sheet of $\frac{1}{8}$-inch-thick birch plywood

Table 16-2. Bill of materials for the tool chest.

BILL OF MATERIALS

Item Number	Description	Quantity	*Vendor Catalogue Number	Vendor Cost	Unit Cost	Total Cost
1	4/4 red oak (S2S to 3/4 inch and S1E)	30				
2	5/8 red oak (S2S to 1/2 inch and S1E)	10				
3	5/8 red oak S2S to 3/8 inch and S1E)	10				
4	4/4 Select D-grade pine	30				
5	3/4-inch oak Shaker knob	22				
6	brass chest lock	1				
7	brass drawer lock	1				
8	bullet catch	2				
9	lid stay	2				
10	blue plush fabric to line drawer bottoms	2				
11	poster board for lining drawer bottoms					
12	can of spray adhesive	1				
	TOTAL COST $					

* If ordering from catalogue

Table 16-3. Sources of supply for the tool chest.

SOURCES OF SUPPLY

Vendor Code	Names and Address	Phone Number

17 BUILDING A WORKBENCH

For most woodcrafters, the workbench is the focal point of their shop. They consider it their most important tool.

The singular purpose of a workbench is to hold the lumber/project while it's being worked on. To this end, the workbench has taken many forms throughout history. Entire books and countless magazine articles have been written on the subject. There are a variety of vises used. The more popular designs include two vises, one located along the front of the tabletop and one on the end.

The workbench described in this chapter and shown in Illus. 17-1 has probably the simplest design. It's little more than a heavy-duty table with a commercially available vise attached. Installing the single vise in an end, or tail, vise helps keep construction cost down while making it capable of holding a fairly large piece of stock.

Workbenches are traditionally made from a tight-grained, hard wood such as beech or maple. There are even some on the market made from exotic species. Since the wood selection can have a significant impact on the cost of the project, common softwoods such as high-grade construction pine or fir could also be used.

This one uses common dimensional lumber found at most lumberyards. Sort through the piles to get the straightest and clearest boards you can. The three -inch-square legs are milled from the conventional 4×4, while the $1\frac{1}{2}$×3-inch stock can be milled from 2×4's. The top is glued up from milled 2×4's. Pay particular attention to the edges of the boards you pull out of the pile at the lumberyard.

CONSTRUCTION PLAN

1. Mill the stock. First trim/joint $\frac{1}{4}$ inch off the edges of the 2×4 tabletop boards. Then trim/joint $\frac{1}{4}$ inch off the edges of the 2×4 apron stock.
2. Glue up the top panel using eight milled pieces.
3. Cut the legs to length.
4. Cut the apron pieces to length.
5. Cut a groove in top of the apron pieces for tabletop fasteners.
6. Form tenons on the apron pieces.
7. Cut mortises in the legs.
8. Assemble the end frame. Peg the mortise-

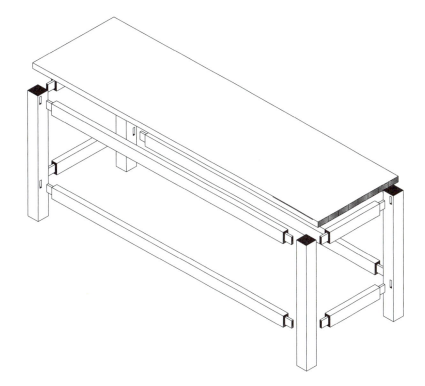

Illus. 17-1. This workbench has a very simple design.

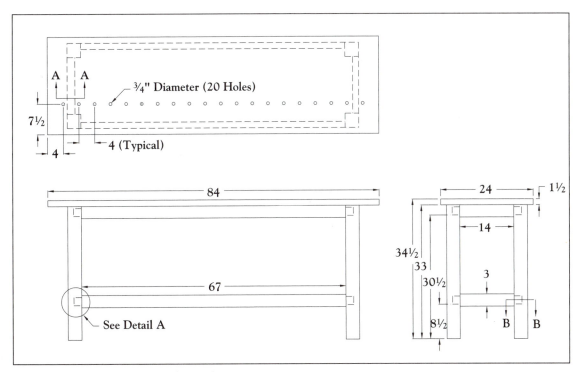

Illus. 17-2. Details for workbench.

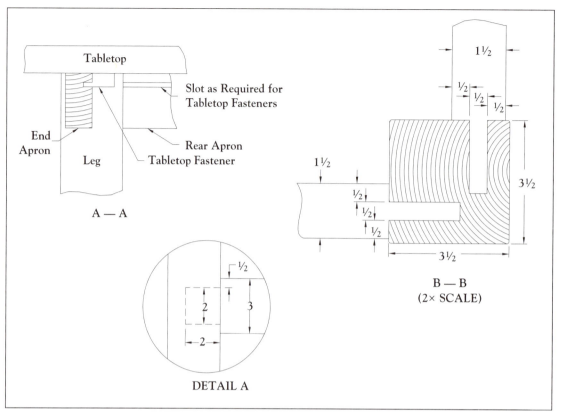

Illus. 17-3. Details for workbench.

and-tenon joints with ⅜-inch dowels. Leave the pegs long, for trimming later.

9. Install the long apron using a mortise-and-tenon joint. Peg the mortise-and-tenon joints with ⅜-inch dowels. Leave the pegs long, for trimming later.
10. Plane/sand the top panel flat and level.
11. Cut the tabletop to length.
12. Locate and bore ¾-inch holes in the top for bench dogs.
13. Trim the pegs flush on the table frame.

14. Temporarily attach the top with a few tabletop fasteners.
15. Temporarily install the vise per the manufacturer's instructions.
16. Remove the vise and permanently install any spacers on the workbench top.
17. Apply several coats of linseed oil finish.
18. Permanently attach the tabletop.
19. Build wooden jaws and attach them to the vise.
20. Permanently install the vise. ◘

Cutting List page 167

Table 17-1. Cutting list for the workbench.

CUTTING LIST

Item Number	Part Name	Quantity	Material	Thickness (inches)	Width (inches)	Length (inches)	Note
	Top Panel	1	Fir	1 ½	24	84	1, 2
	Long Aprons	4	Fir	1 ½	3	72	
	End Aprons	4	Fir	1 ½	3	19	
	Legs	4	Fir	3	3	33	

NOTES:

1. Glue up the top panel using eight 1½×3 -inch boards which have been milled from stud grade or better-grade 2×4 lumber.

2. Trim the top panel to actual size after it has been sanded/planed flat.

18 BUILDING A ROUTER TABLE

The router table is a very popular item used in many operations involving the router. The router is hung upside down under a flat surface with the bit protruding through the surface. In use, the router is held stationary and the work is passed over or along the rotating bit. Router tables must be very stable.

Most router tables on the market are small, table top ones. You might want one with a large enough table surface area to allow you to use panel-raising bits for raised-panel doors.

The table described in this chapter (Illus. 18-1) is large and heavy, to ensure stability. It uses an acrylic insert that simply attaches to the router like the standard router base. The insert then sets in a recess in the tabletop. Such an insert will allow a variety of bit sizes to be used because several plates with varying hole sizes can be added to the recess.

To keep costs down, ordinary construction fir lumber is used for this table. The legs are 4x4 stock; the other parts are made from 2x4 stock. Choose your material carefully. Get boards that are straight and have as few knots as possible. You probably will encounter some

knots in this stock; just be ensure that areas that will have joints are knot-free.

You will probably want to add a simple fence, as shown in Illus. 18-1. Develop your own plan for the fence to match the table. Essentially, all you need for the router table are a base and vertical fence. It would be a good idea to add reinforcements and be absolutely sure that the fence is perpendicular to the router table surface. Plan on the fence resting over the router bit area on occasion. This means notching an area out of the fence, so be careful where you put screws to assemble the unit. Router bits can easily be destroyed by hitting a screw.

Building the router table is really simple. It is very similar to the techniques used for the workbench in the last chapter. It involves the use of mortise-and-tenon joinery to build the table frame. This project also calls for breadboard ends to help keep the top panel stable over the years. If you choose not to use them, which is your call, simply change the dimensions of the top panel and eliminate the breadboard ends.

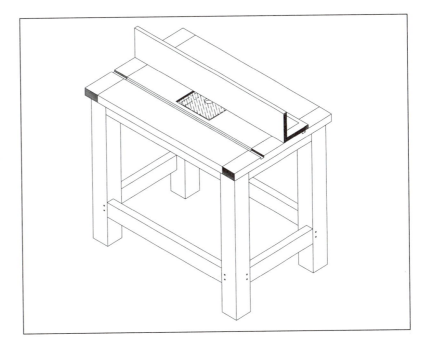

Illus. 18-1. Router table.

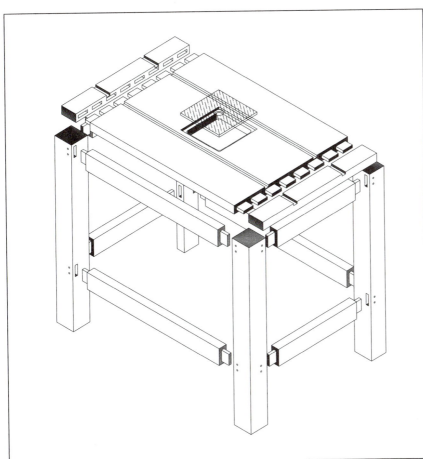

Illus. 18-2.
Exploded view of
the router table.

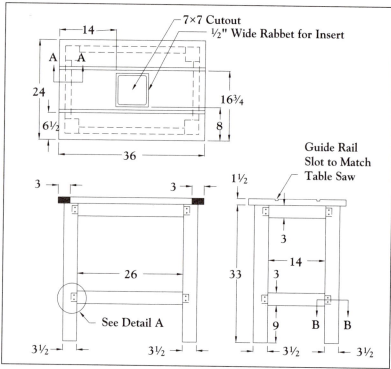

Illus. 18-3. Details for router table.

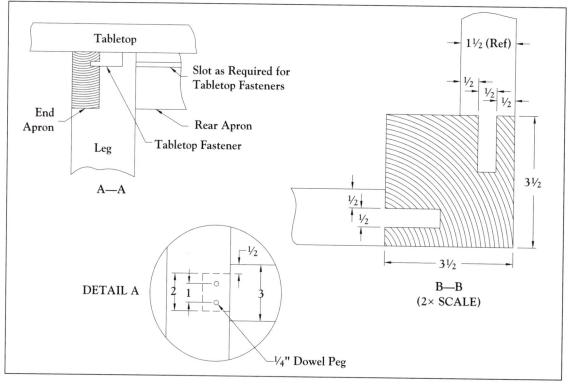

Illus. 18-4. Details for router table.

CONSTRUCTION PLAN

1. Joint and glue up the top panel.
2. Cut the breadboard ends a little oversize.
3. Cut the legs to length.
4. Cut the apron pieces to length. Cut grooves in the top apron pieces for table-top fasteners.
5. Form tenons on the apron pieces.
6. Cut mortises in the legs.
7. Assemble the end frame. Use mortise-and-tenon joints. Pin the mortise-and-tenon joints with $1/4$-inch dowels. Leave the dowels long, for trimming later.
8. Install the long apron using mortise-and-tenon joints.Pin the mortise-and-tenon joints with $1/4$-inch dowels. Leave the dowels long, for trimming later.
9. Plane/sand the top panel flat and level.
10. Cut the tabletop to length.
11. Cut the 7×7 recess or cutout using a sabre saw or keyhole saw close to the lay-out line.
12. Use a straight edge to guide the router while trimming the cutout with a straight bit.
13. Form a $3/8$-inch deep × $1/2$-inch-wide rabbet around the top periphery of the cutout for the acrylic insert. This rabbet can be made with the various rabbet- or slot-cutting bits available on the market.
14. Form the mortise-and-tenon joints on the tabletop panel and the breadboard ends.
15. Attach the breadboard ends, but do not add glue to the tenons, except to the pegs or dowels, which reinforce the joints.
16. Trim the pegs flush with the tabletop.
17. Trim the pegs flush on the frame joints.
18. Apply several coats of linseed oil finish.
19. Attach the tabletop. ▣

Table 18-1. Cutting list for the router table.

CUTTING LIST

Item Number	Part Name	Quantity	Material	Thickness (inches)	Width (inches)	Length (inches)	Note
1	Top Panel	1	Fir	$1\,1/2$	24	33	1, 2
2	Breadboard Ends	2	Fir	$1\,1/2$	3	24	3
3	Long Aprons	4	Fir	$1\,1/2$	3	29	
4	End Aprons	4	Fir	$1\,1/2$	3	17	
5	Legs	4	Fir	$3\,1/2$	$3\,1/2$	33	

NOTES:

1. Glue up the top panel using eight $1\,1/2$×3 -inch boards which have been milled from stud-grade or better 2×4 lumber.
2. Trim the top panel to actual size after sanding/planing it flat.
3. Cut the breadboard ends a little oversize and trim them to match the top panel after it's attached.

19 SHOP AIDS

In this chapter I describe and illustrate how to build a few jigs that will help with many jobs around the shop, especially if you use a table saw. Several jigs call for 1½-inch-thick stock. If you don't have any hardwood of this thickness, sort through your construction lumber pile and select the most knot-free stock you can find. There is no fixed rule requiring hardwood for these projects.

PANEL CUTTER

The first shop project is a table-saw panel cutter (Illus. 19-1). The panel cutter is used as a sliding table when large panels are being crosscut. One of the hazards of crosscutting large or heavy pieces of stock is their tendency to "drag" on the wing extension surface of the table saw. The sliding table will eliminate that problem. It will easily accommodate panels 24 inches wide.

One of the most common questions people ask concerning using a table saw is, "How do I get my cut mark aligned with the blade?" This sliding table panel cutter will give an ideal reference point for the cut mark. I often use a small version in place of the saw's mitre gauge for small stock.

Building the Panel Cutter.

1. Cut the sliding table panel to approximate size. It should be of a sufficient width so that you can reach from the edge of the saw table to a little beyond the blade. (It will be trimmed flush with the blade after the guide rail is attached.)
2. Attach the back stop along the back edge of the sliding panel.
3. Draw a line to position the guide rail on the underside of the panel. Clamp the rail in position while driving screws in from the top. Be *extremely* careful that the rail is perpendicular to the back stop.
4. The longer the guide rail, the less likely there will be much play, so it's best to allow the rail to extend a few inches ahead of the actual sliding table. The guide rail will receive quite a bit of wear over the years. Therefore, it should be made of a hard, dense wood. An occa-

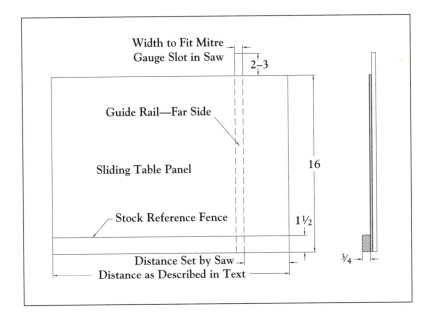

Illus. 19-1. Details for panel cutter.

Width to Fit Mitre Gauge Slot in Saw

2–3

Guide Rail—Far Side

Sliding Table Panel

16

Stock Reference Fence

1½

Distance Set by Saw

Distance as Described in Text

¾

sional application of paraffin will keep the parts moving smoothly.

If you have access to a metalworking shop, you might want to make the guide rail from steel. The most common mitre slot is ¾ inch wide ×⅜ inch deep. This is a common size of steel stock available in larger hardware stores. If you have a drill press and can use a tap, you can make your own steel guide rails.

5. After the rail is in place and checked for square, trim off the end of the panel and back stop by passing the device over the saw blade. From this point forward, any cut will be square. When the layout line is aligned with the edge of the sliding table, it will be guided directly to the saw blade for an accurate cut.

6. Although Illus. 19-1 does not show one, many people will add a vertical dowel or Shaker peg to the back rail to act as a handle.

The panel cutter will slide under most factory-provided blade guards. To use it, simply align the layout mark on the stock to be cut with the edge of the jig. Hold the stock in place on the sliding table and push the jig across the saw

table. Since the edge of the jig was cut by the blade, it will always provide an accurate reference. Take care to prevent any buildup of saw dust in front of the fence. Any debris in this area will prevent your stock from aligning properly and result in misaligned cuts.

A larger jig is excellent for crosscutting wide stock. One advantage of a larger jig is that it will provide you more room for a panel on the saw.

When working with stock thicker than the back stop, it will be necessary to mark the stock on its edge and align that mark with the sliding table.

TENONING JIGS

Tenoning jigs are very useful shop aids. Here I describe how to build two tenoning jigs. The function of the first is to hold a board while the tenon cheeks are cut across the width of the board. Actually, it acts as a carriage which slides along the table-saw rip fence. Illus. 19-2 is a construction drawing for the jig.

A second jig like the one shown in Illus. 19-3 will be used to cut the cheeks across the thickness of the board.

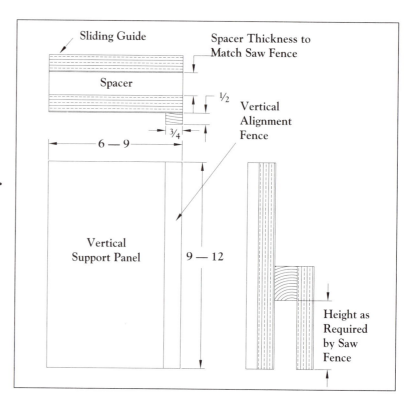

Sliding Guide

Spacer Thickness to Match Saw Fence

Spacer

½

Vertical Alignment Fence

¾

6 — 9

Vertical Support Panel

9 — 12

Height as Required by Saw Fence

Illus. 19–2. Construction drawing of the tenoning jig.

Making the Saddle-Carriage Tenoning Jig

Construction of the saddle-carriage jig is very simple. Since there are so many table saws (and aftermarket rip fences) on the market, you'll need to fine-tune the jig's dimensions to fit your table-saw. Be sure to make it high enough to clear any bolts that might rise above the fence body. It should fit tightly enough against the vertical sides of the rip fence to keep the jig square with the table-saw surface.

Making the Tenoning Jig

To make the jig, do the following:
1. Cut the vertical support panel and sliding guide to size. Note that Illus. 19-2 shows that ¾-inch-thick plywood is used for these parts. This is for better stability.
2. To find the correct spacing, set the two vertical panels to "sandwich" the saw's rip fence and a sheet of paper. The paper

will give an additional allowance to make sure the jig does not "drag" when in use. Mark the gap on the end of a piece of 2×4. The spacer should be at least 1½ inches thick, to allow offsetting rows of screws when the parts are assembled. Make certain the spacer is rip cut absolutely square with the top of the table saw.

3. Clamp the two panels and spacer together as you glue and screw the parts to form the vertical support "saddle." Double-check the vertical support panel to make sure it is vertical to the saw tabletop.
4. Glue and clamp a piece of ½×¾-inch wood in place to form the vertical alignment fence. *Be careful to not use any screws so low as to interfere with the blade when it is raised to its highest elevation.* Use your layout square to make certain that the front edge is vertical to the saw tabletop.

Over time, the lower section of this vertical-alignment fence will be worn away by the saw blade. This is not really a problem as long as enough remains to align workpieces. Also, the boards being worked will still be supported by the upper portion of the jig.

5. A handle of your selection can be added to the back vertical member. Set it in line with the spacer.

Using the Saddle-Carriage Tenoning Jig

1. Using the jig will require the removal of the saw's blade guard, so extreme care is required!

2. *Always* make sure that the board you are working with is cut square. At least the first piece to be worked on must be clearly marked out for setting the blade height and fence location to position the cut.

3. Place the board in the jig. Make sure that its trailing, or back, edge is set against the vertical alignment fence, and it is placed widthwise against the vertical support panel.

4. Clamp the stock in place. You can use spring or C-clamps. If you use C-clamps, be certain to put a piece of scrap between the clamp and stock to prevent the wood from being marred. If you wish, you could make the vertical support fence wide enough to accommodate a toggle clamp, which is permanently mounted to the jig.

5. Bring the stock along the side of the blade and raise the blade to match the layout line on the stock (or the cut for the shoulder if you cut it first).

6. Adjust the location of the fence to align the layout line with the blade. Make sure that the blade is on the "waste" side of the layout line. Always set the cut such that the waste falls away from the workpiece and jig! Otherwise such an error could send a pretty good-sized wood chip flying in your direction at high velocity.

7. Pass the stock over the blade by pushing the tenoning jig slowly.

Making the Second Tenoning Jig

1. Cut the sliding table to size as shown in Illus. 19-3.

2. Cut the vertical fence.

3. Install the guide rails. The guide rails are installed very much like those for the sliding panel cutter. Using two guide rails is completely at your discretion, but it does give better engagement with the table.

   Using a marking square, locate the guide rail. Clamp it in place and secure it with a couple of screws from the top of the sliding table panel. The guide rail can be either a dense-grained hardwood such as maple, beech, or cherry or it could be made from $\frac{3}{8}$ inch $\times$ $\frac{3}{4}$-inch steel bar stock.

4. Install the vertical fence by gluing it and driving screws up through its bottom. Make absolutely certain that the vertical fence is square with the guide rails and is vertical to the saw tabletop. Use two offset rows of screws. *Be sure to locate the area where the saw blade will pass through the jig and keep that area clear of screws.*

5. After the parts of the jig are assembled, set the unit on the table saw and raise the blade an inch or two. Pass the unit over the spinning blade to make the kerf shown in Illus. 19-3. The kerf will give you an excellent reference for aligning your layout lines.

Using the Second Tenoning Jig

Before using this jig, note that depending on the sequence you use to cut the tenon, the markout lines may or may not be there when you need to cut the narrow cheeks on the tenon. To use the jig, do the following:

1. Use the kerf, in the jig, to measure and mark the cheek offset on the jig. Make

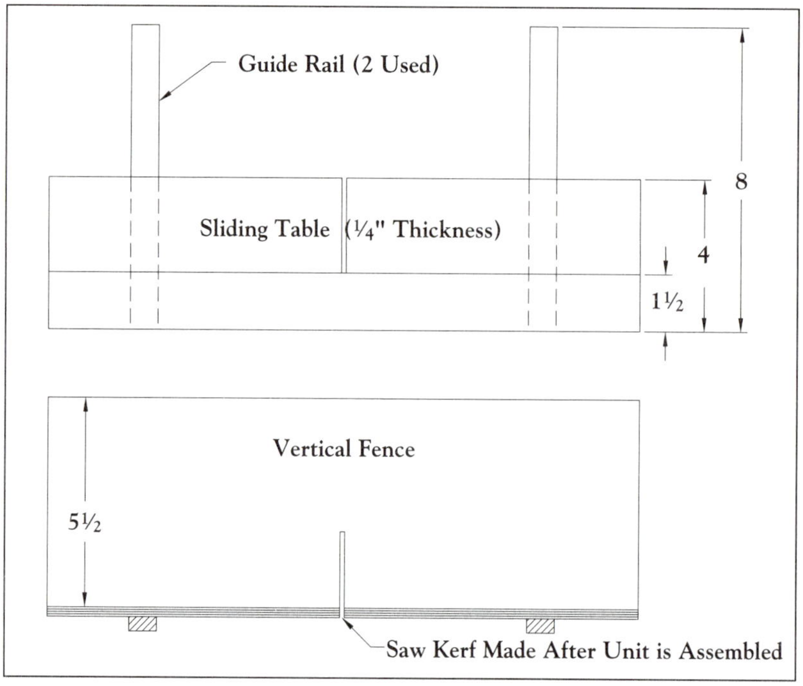

Illus. 19-3. Construction drawing for tenoning jig used to cut the tenon's cheeks across the thickness of the board.

certain that the kerf is on the waste side of the measurement.

2. If you are going to make several tenons, you can clamp a block of wood in place and simply set your workpiece against the block. *Make sure that the block is set on the other side of the workpiece to prevent waste from falling between the block and the workpiece.*

3. After the workpiece is aligned with the jig, clamp it in place and push it slowly over the blade.

TABLE-SAW MITRE JIG

Of all the cuts you make on a table saw, the one which requires the greatest accuracy is the mitre. It's amazing how elusive that 45-degree cut can be.

Here is a jig (Illus. 19-4) that is easy to build and will keep the cuts accurate. It's built similarly to the sliding table panel cutter. Other than the mitre fences, the primary difference between this jig and the panel cutter is the table for this jig is larger. This is to accommodate the mitre fences supporting both pieces to

be joined. The spanning rail along the back of the jig keeps the two table halves connected and acts as a handle. Actually, the jig should never have to be passed over the blade beyond the mitre fences.

Making the Mitre Jig

1. Start building the mitre jig by cutting the sliding table panel. For stability, use ¾-inch-thick material. Make sure it is square. Mark a centerline from the front edge of the panel to the back. This layout line should align with the middle of the saw blade. Using this line as a reference, cut two dadoes to match the mitre-gauge slots on the table saw. Install guide rails to fit the dadoes. Again, if you prefer, you could use steel guide rails.

2. The next step is to lay out the mitre fences. As shown in Illus. 19-5, draw a baseline, parallel with the back of the sliding table. Make sure that the distance to the edge will allow for the spanning rail. Mark a point on the centerline

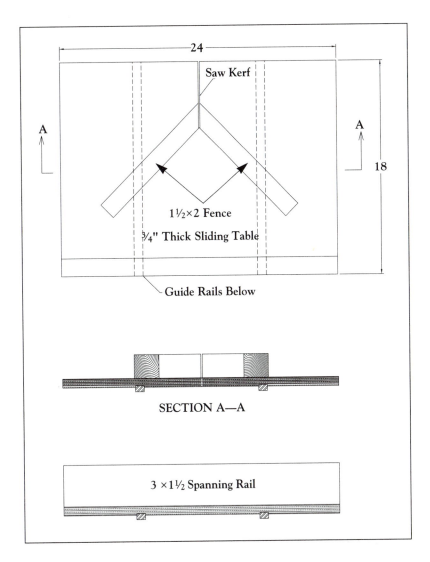

Illus. 19-4. Mitring jig.

a distance away from the baseline equal to one half the length of the baseline. Draw lines connecting this mark with the ends of the baseline.

The result of this exercise in geometry is a right triangle cut in half by the original centerline. Very carefully, attach a mitre fence aligned with either mitre line. Let the fence stock extend beyond the centerline, but do not attach it with glue or screws beyond that point.

3. Pass the jig over the blade of the saw. Do not go past the mitre fence any farther than necessary. This will trim off the first fence and set you up to install the second. Use the first mitre fence to trim off a piece of stock for the second fence.

4. To attach the second mitre fence, simply set a carpenter's square (checked for accuracy) against the first fence and use it to locate the second fence. Simply butt the mitred end of the second fence against that of the first and glue/screw it in place on the sliding table. Pass the jig over the blade again; this will create a saw kerf between the two fences. This kerf can be

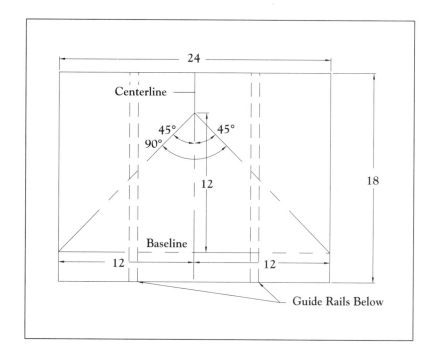

Illus. 19-5. Mitre fence's layout.

used to position the stock just as on the panel-cutting jig described earlier.

Using the Mitre Jig

1. When using the mitre jig, remember that the stock will tend to slide along the mitre fence, even as you are making the cut. Whenever possible, either clamp your stock to the fences or glue a strip of sandpaper to the fence to keep the stock from sliding as you hold it in place with your hand.

   You should never push the jig completely through the saw blade separating the sliding table into two pieces. The jig should stop moving as soon as the mitre fences clear the blade.

2. Also remember that the mitre fences should be square with one another. Use one of the fences for one part of the mitre joint, and the other fence for the other part of the mitred joint. This is because *any* inaccuracy in placement of the first mitre fence will be apparent in

the joint. However, as long as the mitre fences are at 90-degree angles to one another, the error will not be apparent.

TABLE-SAW TAPERING JIG

Tapering stock is called for fairly often in carcass furniture and for table legs. The tapering jig shown in Illus. 19-6 is for use on table saws and is adjustable to accommodate an infinite variety of tapers. It's fairly straightforward to build.

As you can see from Illus. 19-6, you'll need two pieces of straight wood. You might be tempted to screw the hinge into the end. This would be a mistake, because the end grain will not take screws very securely. They need to cut across the grain. This tapering jig incorporates a dowel (available at many woodworking supply outlets) for use as a handle.

Building the Tapering Jig

1. Cut the two boards to dimension. Make sure that the width of the boards will be

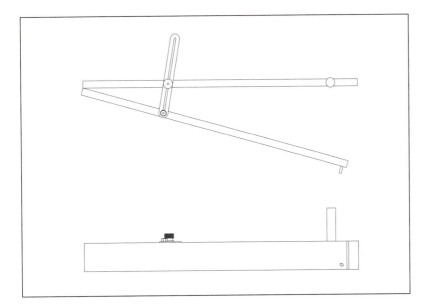

Illus. 19-6. Tapering jig.

higher than the saw's fence.

2. Drill a hole and install a piece of dowel to act as a stop.
3. Install the hinge. Be sure to recess the hinge leaf so that the two parts of the jig will be flush when closed.
4. Drill a hole for the Shaker peg handle.
5. Glue the Shaker peg in the jig board.
6. Attach a heavy-duty lid support, placing the fixed end on the part that will pivot away from the saw's rip fence. This will prevent the lid support from interfering with the stock being machined.
7. Install a hanger bolt (sized to fit the lid support). Use your preference for either a polished brass thumb nut or common wing nut to secure the lid support when the taper has been established.
8. Establish a mark on top of the piece with the stop dowel, and another mark 12 inches towards the front of the jig on both parts. In the future, you will establish taper angles by measuring the distance between the two boards at these marks. With one inch between boards at this point, the taper will be one inch per foot.

Using the Taper Jig

1. The table-saw safety guard will have to be removed when you are using the taper jig. Always make safety your top priority.
2. Set the taper and tighten the adjusting nut.
3. Set the saw fence such that the forward edge of the bevel is aligned with the blade.
4. Always use a push stick to hold the material in place in the jig and use its handle when pushing the jig over the blade.

FINGER-JOINT JIG

The finger joint is described in Chapter 3. It is used in some utilitarian carcasses, boxes, and drawers. As discussed earlier, the finger-joint jig can be used on either a table saw or router table. The jig (Illus. 19-7 and 19-8) is set for a single joint size.

Building the Finger-Joint Jig

1. Cut the sliding table and fixed fence to size. The upright fences need to be high enough to provide a solid support while

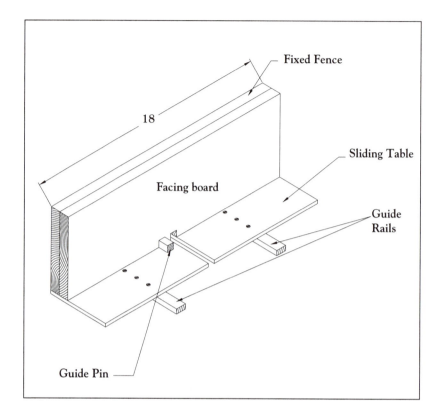

Illus. 19-7. Finger- or box-joint jig.

Fixed Fence

Sliding Table

Facing board

Guide Rails

Guide Pin

18

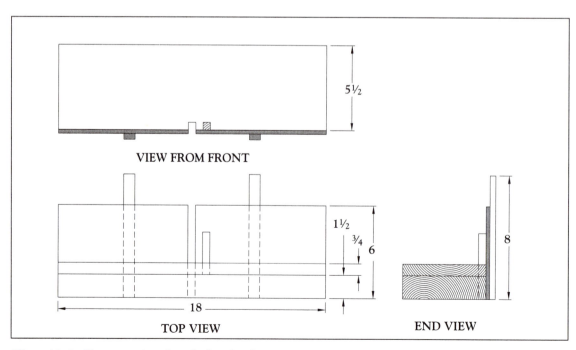

VIEW FROM FRONT

5½

TOP VIEW

END VIEW

18

1½

¾

6

8

Illus. 19-8. Construction details for the finger-joint jig.

the work is moved over the table saw.

2. Install the guide rails. These have to be made from a hard, dense hardwood such as maple or cherry. You could also use steel if you have access to a metalworking facility.

   Make sure that the guide rails are perpendicular to the fences.

3. After the guide rails are in place, clamp the facing board to the fixed fence.

4. Using either a table saw or a router table, raise the cutter so that it is just above the sliding table and pass the jig over the cutter.

5. Adjust the cutter height to about $1/64$ inch higher than the thickness of the wood you will be joining. (Measure above the sliding table surface.)

6. Pass the jig over the cutter to complete cutting the notch in the vertical fences.

7. Cut a piece of hard stock that fits in the notch created in the last step. This will eventually become the guide pin. It's a good idea to make it 9 to 12 inches long for now and cut a 1 -inch piece off to use as a spacer. This piece of wood should fit in the notch as tightly as possible.

8. Remove the clamps you used to hold the facing board in place on the vertical fence and separate the two pieces.

9. Glue a section of the guide pin in place in the facing board It is a good idea to allow it to be long enough to allow several pieces of stock to be machined simultaneously. Do not allow the guide pin to protrude beyond the back surface of the facing board .

10. Set the basic jig in place with the facing board on the table saw or router table.

11. Move the jig such that the vertical fence is pretty close to the cutter.

12. Use the small section of the guide pin you cut earlier to space the actual guide pin from the cutter. Setting this spacing is critical because any error will be multiplied times the number of fingers you have in the joint you are making. The two parts you are assembling with the box joint may not even fit together.

13. Clamp the two fences together again, after setting the spacing, and run the jig assembly over the cutter to cut another notch in the adjustable fence.

14. *Carefully* measure the width of the notch you just cut and the spacing between it and the guide pin. It might take a couple of tries setting the fence to get the spacing precise.

15. When the spacing is set, lock the fence in place by driving several screws through it and into the vertical fence.

    Using the finger or box-joint jig is covered in detail in Chapter 3.

RIPPING CARRIAGE

The rip fence of a table saw is only functional when the edge of the board being guided by it is straight. Although many hardwood suppliers can, and will, supply your lumber SlS (Straight One Side), you will run into the occasional outlet that does not possess the equipment. Also, buying the wood SlS will raise its cost. The cost increase is really quite small considering the time involved in doing it yourself. This ripping carriage (Illus. 19-9) will help to ensure that the edge of the board the rip fence is guiding is straight.

Making the Rip Jig

1. Cut the jig base to size as shown in Illus. 19-9.

2. Make a guide rail to fit the mitre slot of your table saw. Use either a dense hardwood or steel.

3. Attach the guide rail to the bottom of the base. Locate it such that the edge of the base will be trimmed by the saw. This will give you a reference when placing your lumber on the jig.

4. Cut the back stop and glue/screw it in place as shown in Illus. 19-9.

5. Set either a small nail or screw in the back stop. Clip the nail off at an angle or file the screw to form a point. This will be used to help hold the wood you are

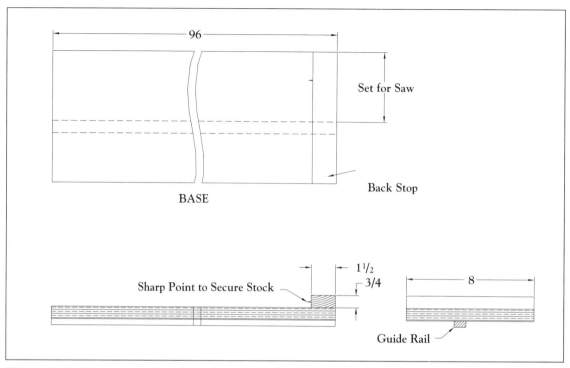

Illus. 19-9. Ripping carriage.

ripping in place on the jig.

6. Glue either a strip of sandpaper from a sanding belt (medium to coarse) or several sheets of sandpaper on the jig. Again, this will help keep the stock from sliding around.

Using the Ripping Jig

The jig can be used with most standard table-saw blade guards in place. To use it, do the following:

1. Set the stock to be cut on the jig and drive it onto the point formed by the nail or screw you put into the back stop. Allow the edge you want to straighten to overhang the edge of the jig formed by passing the jig over the blade during construction.

2. Press down on the stock so the sandpaper "grabs" the stock and push the jig over the saw, guided by the guide rail in the table saw's mitre slot.

3. After one edge is straightened, the board can be ripped to width by running the straight edge along the saw's rip fence. ◘

INDEX

INDEX

Metric Conversion Table

INCHES TO MILLIMETRES AND CENTIMETRES

MM—*millimetres*   CM—*centimetres*

Inches	MM	CM	Inches	CM	Inches	CM
⅛	3	0.3	9	22.9	30	76.2
¼	6	0.6	10	25.4	31	78.7
⅜	10	1.0	11	27.9	32	81.3
½	13	1.3	12	30.5	33	83.8
⅝	16	1.6	13	33.0	34	86.4
¾	19	1.9	14	35.6	35	88.9
⅞	22	2.2	15	38.1	36	91.4
1	25	2.5	16	40.6	37	94.0
1¼	32	3.2	17	43.2	38	96.5
1½	38	3.8	18	45.7	39	99.1
1¾	44	4.4	19	48.3	40	101.6
2	51	5.1	20	50.8	41	104.1
2½	64	6.4	21	53.3	42	106.7
3	76	7.6	22	55.9	43	109.2
3½	89	8.9	23	58.4	44	111.8
4	102	10.2	24	61.0	45	114.3
4½	114	11.4	25	63.5	46	116.8
5	127	12.7	26	66.0	47	119.4
6	152	15.2	27	68.6	48	121.9
7	178	17.8	28	71.1	49	124.5
8	203	20.3	29	73.7	50	127.0